Skater Girl

Skater Girl

A Girl's Guide to Skateboarding

Patty Segovia
Rebecca Heller

Ulysses Press

Published by:
ULYSSES PRESS
P.O. Box 3440
Berkeley, CA 94703
www.ulyssespress.com

ISBN10: 1-56975-542-6
ISBN13: 978-1-56975-542-6
Library of Congress Control Number 2006900289

Printed in Canada by Transcontinental Printing

10 9 8 7 6 5 4 3 2 1

Acquisitions Editor: Ashley Chase
Managing Editor: Claire Chun
Editor: Lily Chou
Production: Matt Orendorff, Steven Schwartz
Design: what!design @ whatweb.com
Cover Photos: © Patty Segovia
Interior photos: © Patty Segovia except on page 39 (Cara-Beth Burnside); pages 40, 53, 62 (Heidi Fitzgerald); pages 54, 55, 56 (Kervin Krause); and page 116 (Gravity Skateboards/Michael Bream)

Distributed by Publishers Group West

Anyone who practices the techniques in this book does so at her own risk and should wear appropriate safety equipment, especially a helmet. The authors and the publisher assume no responsibility for the use or misuse of information contained in this book or for any injuries that may occur as a result of practicing the techniques contained herein. The illustrations and text are for informational purposes only. It is imperative to practice these techniques with the utmost safety in mind. Additionally, one should consult a physician before embarking on any demanding physical activity.

Contents

Foreword
by Cara-Beth Burnside

The first time I saw girls skateboarding changed my life. I was ten and enthralled with roller skating. That all changed after a new skate park opened near my home.

I'd seen boys skateboarding in my neighborhood. Some had even visited my elementary school and put on a skateboarding demonstration. But it wasn't until I saw a team of girls dropping in and carving that I could envision myself on a skateboard. I ditched the eight wheels and switched to four.

I purchased my first skateboard with birthday money and started skating constantly. The guys in the neighborhood would say, "Girls can't skate," but all they did was make me more determined. My dad gave me a summer pass to the skate park, and I showed them girls could skate—everyday, all day. Eventually, my skills blew away plenty of the boys. It was great.

When I got older, I started to compete with and against guys. There were a few girls I skateboarded with, but not many. I loved skateboarding so much and was bummed when I began to realize there was no future for me in skateboarding. The teams didn't want to send me anywhere. It felt hopeless.

I got into snowboarding and started to get flowed free stuff. I competed in contests and made a living and traveled the world. So I got good—I even came in fourth in the 1998 Olympics. But I never stopped skateboarding.

Things began to change in 1997 when the All Girl Skate Jam first took place. ESPN and Fox came out for the first time to interview and film us skating. We even had a $4,000 prize purse. The contest was history in the making for girl skateboarders. It was cool to skate with so many other ladies for the first time and receive support from spectators and media. People came to watch us—girls—skateboard. Receiving TV exposure eventually helped us get sponsors.

The female skate scene began gaining momentum. Patty Segovia's hard work with the All Girl Skate Jam helped make it happen. I'm thankful and happily congratulate Patty for next year's 10th anniversary with AGSJ.

I love skateboarding with other girls, and I'm stoked to see a book that gives girls helpful hints and tips to help them get started. Anything that encourages girls to skate is a good thing.

If a little girl gets feedback like "that's cool," "keep skating" and "let me film you," she's going to go far in skate-

Cara-Beth (left) with amateur skater Ciara D'Agostino.

boarding. Positive affirmation will only push her further if she competes, gets exposure and has the support of her parents. The more girls' skateboarding magazines and videos she has to look at, the better.

This book and other outlets for girls skateboarding keep girls inspired and charging ahead. Progress prevents girls from getting bored (no pun intended).

The sport needs to continue advancing to stimulate skaters to challenge themselves.

If, when I was younger, I had walked into a skate shop and saw ten girls' magazines and videos to look at, my entire world could've been different. Today's professional female skaters and all-girl contests are helping. They already set the standard and girls don't hesitate to believe they can be like female pro skateboarders, but better.

People who love skateboarding live to skate. We get in a zone and nothing else matters. Sometimes we're oblivious to what else is going on in the world—we're that focused. It's not like that every session, but those are the moments I love about skateboarding. Learning a new trick is the best high.

You need to teach yourself to skate, and this book can help you get started. And don't forget to watch other skateboarders. Protective equipment is essential—I know. I've had concussions and sprained my wrist. As an athlete, take what you do seriously. Make sure to eat well, stretch and take care of your health.

For now, I just really want to skate and help women in skateboarding. I'm trying to focus on what I can do to help facilitate change or do something positive for skateboarding. I want to give back. Through the organization of female skaters I created, Action Sports Alliance, better know as "the Alliance," I and other female skaters strive to raise the exposure of women's skateboarding, obtain mainstream sponsors and increase contest money.

Now it's time for you to start skating. Become a part of it. Welcome.

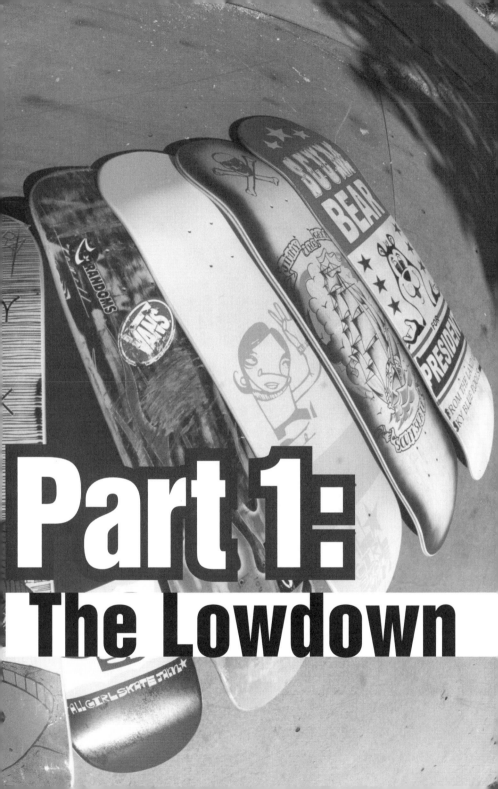

Part 1:
The Lowdown

Chapter 1:
Top 10 Reasons Why Skate- boarding Rocks!

As soon as you experience the thrill of sliding in control or being weightless, you'll realize skateboarding is absolutely the best activity ever. Here are ten other reasons why.

1. Skateboarding is free. One of the best things about skateboarding is that it doesn't cost anything to skate—it's totally *free!* Sure, you might pay anywhere from $4 to $15 to skate at your local skate park, but hitting the street, sliding downhill, or dropping into an empty backyard pool costs you absolutely nothing. That's the magic of skating—you have the freedom to choose what you want to do and when you want to do it. Skateboarding can be done anytime, anywhere.

2. Skateboarding is a sport anyone can enjoy. Skateboarding embraces every gender, race, religion and even ability level. Skating is all about *you*. You are your only obstacle and your best

> **Hint:** A great idea for beginners is to watch other skaters, either in the park or in skate videos. Check out their style and abilities. You can learn a lot from watching others.

<<<

cheerleader. As you learn how to balance on a skateboard, you'll see how easy it is to skate. Getting good is easier than you think. If at first you don't succeed, try, try again. It's like anything you do in life—the more you practice, the better you'll get. You can excel in skating as long as you're willing to put in the time. It's fun and easy to learn!

3. Skateboarding is safe. According to the 2003 Consumer Product Safety Review, more injuries occur in sports like basketball, football and bicycling than skateboarding. More and more skate parks are opening around the country, giving skaters safe, traffic-free places to skate. Protective equipment made specifically for skateboarding, such as helmets, knee, elbow and wrist pads, has come a long way over the years by using the best technology avail-

able. By using equipment properly, you can reduce the risk of injury and spend more time doing what you love—skateboarding.

4. Girl time. You may prefer to learn with a group of girls, especially when you're starting out—it can be a lot less intimidating and may help boost your skating abilities. Once you set out to skate with your girlfriends a couple of times a week, you'll realize that the support girls provide each other will push each skater to improve. Something about skating with the same gender helps you connect and encourages you to try new things. Arranging an all-girls' night at a local skate park is a super fun idea. Or how about starting a skateboarding club at your school? Did I hear "Skate PE?"

5. Skateboarding is healthy and organic. Skating is an excellent cardiovascular activity that's great for your heart and keeps your muscles toned. Sweating will make you feel fantastic. Your adrenaline is pumping—you're on a natural high—and you won't even feel the workout until after you've stopped skating. Plus, skating is organic, and it allows you to express yourself by letting you create your own tricks. "Creativity" is an essential word in a skateboarder's vocabulary.

>>> "As a speed fiend experienced in both, I prefer slalom. The feeling of the wind in my face and the sense of accomplishment I get when I complete a difficult course are two of the many reasons I keep racing. There is also a strong camaraderie among the slalom 'family.'"

—Lynn Kramer, 2005 Slalom World Champion

6. Skateboarding is not a crime. In the past, skateboarding was seen as a rebellious activity, and society held a negative view of skaters. That's all changing now. Competitions like the All Girl Skate Jam, the X-Games, and the Slam City Jam have brought skateboarding into the mainstream. Sprint video cellphone features "The Street TV" girl's skateboarding, and even Ronald McDonald is a fan of skateboarding. The skateboarding industry is preparing itself for a big skateboarding demo at the 2008 Olympics. Imagine that: Skateboarding in the Olympics—and, if we have anything to say about it, it'll include girl skaters! What a major historical accomplishment. Skating has certainly come a long way, baby!

7. Skateboarding keeps you out of trouble. Have you ever seen those T-shirts that say, "Skateboarding saved my life"? Some people say skateboarding helped them stop smoking or lose weight. Skateboarding boosts self-confidence and can even develop mental clarity due to a major release of endorphins. Simply said, skateboarding gets you stoked!

8. Good vibrations. Skateboarding attracts the coolest people, and each one is unique. There are thrill skaters, business skaters, jock skaters, school skaters, part-time skaters, social skaters, poser skaters, recreational skaters, innovative skaters, trendsetter skaters, activist skaters, yoga skaters, surfer skaters and, of course, GIRL SKATERS! All skaters, no matter how different they are, have something in common: they love to travel, explore new skate terrain, and meet others who share their excitement about skateboarding.

9. Super sick styles. Nowadays, skate equipment and clothing are *sweet*! Back in the old days, we only had boys' clothing to choose from—either baggy pants or over-sized shorts. The decks had graphics on them that were either too masculine or just plain insulting to women. Today, companies offer the coolest clothing and accessories for girls. Skate equipment designed espe-cially for the ladies includes everything from stylish boards and helmets to personalized leopard or funky-colored protective pads. Pop into a skate or surf shop and check out the great array of girls' clothing brands.

10. Skateboarding is weatherproof. It doesn't matter the season, you can always skate. Rain? Snow? Street heat so high you could cook an egg on the asphalt? No problem—just head to an indoor skate park and skate to your heart's content. Too much or not enough snow can keep you off your snowboard, and high winds or no waves can keep you from the surf. But skating? We've got that going year-round. After all, a girl can only do so much shopping.

Chapter 2:
Your Skateboard

Alright, Skater Girl, now it's time to get a board. But how do you know what kind of skateboard to buy? Well, this chapter will tell you all you need to know.

It's important to pick out the right equipment for your developing style, so you need to know a little something about the components of a skateboard. A skateboard has four main parts: the deck (the board you stand on), the wheels, the trucks (which connect the wheels to the board and allow the board to turn) and the bearings (they go inside the wheels and allow them to spin). Skateboards range in size and shape for different kinds of riding.

As a beginner, it's easiest to purchase a complete package (deck, trucks and wheels) that is already put together. These are called, curiously enough, "completes." As you improve, you'll find which brands of components work best for you, but it's fine to start out with a pre-assembled board from a skate shop. When heading into a store, don't be afraid or embarrassed to let them know you are new to this sport. Also, don't let those boys at the skate shop intimidate you. You're not a pro yet, but you could be some day!

A skateboard package should cost $100 to $175 dollars (if it costs less, you're almost certainly getting less). It's VERY important to buy a board from a reputable manufacturer or to go to a dedicated skate shop with knowledgeable staff to help you buy a quality ride. Don't pick some unknown brand at a toy store or other general goods store. You get what you pay for and skateboards from toy stores are just that: toys. You or your parents may see the price tag and think the skateboard looks great, but cheaply made skateboards can be dangerous. The wheels may be made of plastic instead of urethane and this will cause them to stick. Also, plastic trucks might not hold up under stress and could break while you're riding or performing tricks, possibly leading to injury. Keep in mind that you're doing most of your riding on asphalt, so you want to have the safest and most stable equipment possible (right, Mom?). You're risking your safety by buying cheap skateboards or parts for your board. (Plus, you might feel like a kook when you show up at the skate park on your Target board.) It's wiser to invest money in your board than into a trip to the emergency room.

>>> If you don't want to sink a bunch of money into a board until you're sure about what you want, you can probably borrow your first board until you decide the style of skateboard that's right for you. I'm sure the boys in your neighborhood would be stoked if you asked them to demo their board.

Can you buy a used skateboard or use a hand-me-down? Sure, but be sure to check it out carefully before committing. Make sure there are no cracks in the deck or trucks (wear in the wheels is okay since these are the cheapest things to replace).

THE PARTS

Let's talk about the different parts of your skateboard:

Deck

The type of skateboarding you want to do will help you determine what kind of deck you should get. If you're looking to do tricks on the street, you want to look for a street deck. Thinking of charging the half-pipe? Then you'll want a slightly bigger, more concave board. If you just want to seriously cruise distances or bomb hills, a longboard might be best for you. You don't necessarily need to buy all three boards at the beginning. If all of the above sound interesting to you, one good board can get you started. Most likely your first purchase will be a street deck, and you'll see where that leads you. However, as you become a better skater, you may find you want specific boards for specific styles of riding.

Skateboard decks are made from thin layers of maple wood, which is strong and flexible. The layers are pressed together with glue. After a few days of curing, the final shape is cut out, the edges are sanded and the graphics are silk-screened. Some skate shops have decks called "blanks." These are decks with little or no graphics on them and they are less expensive than brand-

name boards. This is one place where you can save money without sacrificing quality.

Standard skateboards normally have a width of 7 to 8.5 inches and a length of 29 to 34 inches. The smaller boards may be easier for you to control and easier for performing flip tricks. Wider boards have a larger surface, so they provide more balance. Most boards have the same nose and tail width but the trucks are placed slightly differently. Because it's hard to tell the nose from the tail when looking down at a skate-board, some riders (even the pros) will place a piece of colored grip tape or a different colored screw to mark it. You could also take a rock and make an "X" on the nose of your board.

The curvature of a skateboard deck is called the "concave." When it's shaped, the deck is sort of scooped like a spoon and this actually makes the board stronger. Plus, it lets you know where to place your feet and helps you control the ride. "Mellow" or shallow concaves, where the edges of the board don't come up too high, are good for street and technical tricks, as they are designed to flip more easily. "Steep" or deeper concaves are often used for ramp and pool skating.

Most boards offer a certain amount of flex or bend. When you put weight on the center of the board, you can feel it give a little. The flex will absorb impact from a jump or drop, helps make a ride over a rough surface smoother, and allows the board to make sharper turns.

Try out a couple of boards and see what works best for you.

>>> FIND IT NOW: Decks

AGSJ Skateboards
www.allgirlskatejam.com

Cool Girls Skateboards
www.coolgirlsskateboards.com

Curly Grrlz Skateboards
www.curlygrrlz.com

Element Skateboards
www.elementskateboards.com

Powell Skateboards
www.powellskateboards.com

Rookie Skateboards
www.rookieskateboards.com

Santa Cruz Skateboards
www.santacruzskateboards.com

Santa Monica Airlines
www.smaskateboards.com

Termite Skateboards
www.termiteskateboards.com

Longboards are skateboards made for "cruising," and the ride may feel more like surfing. They're usually 36 inches or longer and are shaped differently than regular skateboards. In fact, they may look more like surfboards. Longboards are a lot longer and some may be wider. The nose and tail vary greatly—some have a concave nose and a square tail, while others have short noses and long pintails (where the tail comes together at a point). Longboards are great for cruising along a flat stretch because they get more glide per push than a regular board. Or you can bomb down a hill, carving back and forth for a great long ride. Gravity, Sector 9 and Arbor are all reputable companies that sell longboards to females. They feature feminine graphics and are just as durable as their "boy" skateboards.

FIND IT NOW: Longboards <<<

Arbor Sports
www.arborsports.com

Gravity Skateboards
www.gravityboard.com

Sector 9
www.sector9.com

All decks are, or will need to be, covered with grip tape (black, rough sandpaper surface on one side and sticky glue on the other), which is applied to the top of the deck so that your feet grip while riding. You can personalize your board by decorating it with stencils or using art markers to draw and paint on your grip tape.

Wheels

The four wheels on your board are crucial to your riding experience. The two classifications for skateboard wheels are durometer and size. Wheel hardness is measured in *durometer* and this can fall anywhere from 87A to 100A; the higher the durometer, the harder the wheel. Soft wheels (87A) give a smoother ride that's ideal for cruising, while harder wheels (100A) might be better for street skaters. In the pool or ramp, you may want to start with a more gripping wheel (95A) but later change to a harder wheel. Because durometer can be confusing, some wheel manufactures (such as Bones) use other naming methods, such as STF (street tech formula) and SPF (skate park formula).

The *size* of the wheel is measured in millimeters and can range from 52mm to 78mm. The size of the wheels will relate to your board:

smaller boards have smaller wheels, while larger boards have bigger, wider wheels. Large, soft wheels, like those you may see on a longboard, generally go faster and have more grip. Smaller, harder wheels are lightweight, making the board easier to perform tricks on.

Quality wheels are made of a urethane formula, which is a hard rubber substance that performs well on different surfaces. Every wheel is different and you may want to try out different kinds as you improve. The goal is to find ones that will last and give you a smooth ride. Unfortunately, cool colors or awesome graphics are not the basis for what kind of wheel you should choose. Instead, you need to pick your wheels by where or on what you'll be riding. Beginners may want to start with a larger wheel with a softer durometer that will be more forgiving on rough surfaces and last longer. You can only have wheels that are so big before

>>> Before urethane wheels were first used in 1973, metal and clay wheels were the norm but provided no grip. Urethane offered riders a smoother, quieter and more stable ride. And did you know a woman named Uma Chowdry invented tethatrane, a chemical used to make urethane? Cool.

getting "wheel bite" (when the deck and wheels touch as you turn the board, causing you to bail big time!). To avoid this, you can add plastic or rubber cushions, called "risers," that go between the deck and truck. Ask your friends and skate shop employees for advice or feel free to e-mail the girls over at All Girl Skate Jam (www.allgirlskatejam.com).

Trucks

The trucks hold the wheels on to the board and allow the wheels to turn. The parts of a truck are the base plate, king-pin, axle, hanger and bushing. The *base plate* is the plate that gets bolted down to your board. The *kingpin* connects the hanger and the base plate. You can adjust the kingpin to make your trucks looser or tighter. On any quality board the kingpin will be countersunk so that it won't get in the way of the skater's grind. The *axles* are imbedded into the *hanger*, which is the part of the truck for grinding. Your wheels attach to the axle. The *bush-ings* give the trucks some cushion, allowing the board to turn. As the bushings on your trucks loosen up, they start to feel different; you can tighten them with a skate tool or wrench. If and when your bushings begin to deteriorate, they

can be replaced for only a couple bucks at your skate shop.

Again, the kind of skating you do will determine the kind of trucks you want. Durable trucks should be used if you're planning on grinding. Skating street or grinding pools will usually wear your trucks down a lot quicker than skating other terrain. Make sure your trucks are not too loose or too tight because this can really affect your riding. It can be compared to the handlebars on your bike—if they are too loose you will ride squirrelly (all over the place). You want to have a great first experience so that you're eager to return to another skate session the very next day.

When looking at a new board, make sure the trucks aren't plastic. It's also best to check for a reputable name stamped into the plate (names such as Independent, Tracker, Venture, Thunder or Grind King are all good signs of a quality truck).

>>> **Tip:** To put your bearing into your wheel, place your skateboard on its side. Put two bearings on the axle. Press the wheel down on the axle with both hands so that it slips over one of the bearings. Once the bearing is in on one side, flip the wheel over and do it again to press in the second bearing.

Bearings

Bearings sit between the wheel and the axle and allow the wheels to spin. The bearings encase 6 to 7 separate balls. Bearings are rated by speed. A lower-rated bearing (ABEC 5) is good for beginners. There are two bearings per skate wheel and you can use your skate tool to insert these bearings a lot easier.

Bearings must be kept out of dirt, sand and water or they'll get ruined and no longer turn. Think of bearings as your bike chain—it'll rust and not work properly if water or dirt gets inside it.

Nuts and bolts

The nuts and bolts hold the board together. Randoms, Khiro and Shorty's are quality, well-known brands. Randoms even makes custom bolts with images such as skull designs and more. Skateboard bolts are specifically made out of high-grade steel. They are better than the bolts you may find at a hardware store.

CARE

So you just dropped more than $100 on your new skateboard. Rule #1: Don't let it disappear. Keep it under your feet, indoors or in the car. Don't leave it outside the coffee shop or skate store if you're planning on riding home.

When not riding, keep your skateboard indoors or in the garage—and make sure it's someplace dry. If you leave it outside, it could rust or become soggy with water damage and ruin your ride by taking away the "pop," or flex.

Tip: Riders who are small and <<< light may want to consider a "mini." These skateboards have a length that's between 26 and 27 inches and a width of about 6 or 7 inches.

Before you head out, always check your board over to make sure the nuts and bolts are tight (you shouldn't be able to turn them with your fingers) and that the wheels spin smoothly. Every couple of weeks or months, depending on use, rotate your wheels by taking them off the board, flipping the outside to the inside and putting them in a different position (for instance, the former left front wheel now goes on the right back truck). Replace wheels when they "flatspot," or flatten in only one area from overuse.

If your board or trucks break or crack, it's time to replace them. "Razortail," when the nose or tail becomes sharp from skidding, is normal, but when the tail gets too thin or the board starts to chip, think about getting a new deck.

Sometimes you may get a little dirt on your board, which can lessen your grip. What should you do? You can try to blow it off or rub it with a stiff brush. Grip-tape erasers are also available; they work pretty well for removing the dirt.

Clean your bearings by wiping them with a cloth and applying some grease or speed cream. For a super-clean bearing, use hot water and compressed air to dry, then apply speed cream.

Chapter 3:
First Time:
Tips for Success

So you've found a skateboard (whether you stole one from your brother, borrowed one from your friend or bought one) and now you're ready to hit the pavement. But what's a girl to wear? Where to go? What to do?

WHAT TO WEAR

Okay, we know that there's no official uniform for skater girls, but there are a couple of sensible things that will help the beginner so she doesn't get too thrashed by the pavement the first couple of times out. You may look cute in just your bikini top, shorts, and flip-flops—but until you've mastered sidewalk surfing, you're going to need to wear protective gear and sensible shoes.

Shoes

Sneakers! There, we've said it. While they might not be the girliest pair of shoes in your closet, sneakers are a must for skateboarding. Luckily, these days, manufacturers have come out with cool lines of skate sneakers made specifically for women so you don't have to get men's kicks in small sizes. In fact,

most of the people who wear skate shoes probably don't even own a board. You should have no trouble finding a pair in your favorite color and in a style you like. However, be careful to buy true skate-specific shoes instead of cheaply made "skater-looking" shoes that may come apart when put to the test. Some brands that make skate shoes for girls are Vans, DVS, Etnies and DC. You can find these shoes at skate shops or department stores (or you may even find a better deal on these quality brands online).

For ramp skating or cruising, look for shoes that don't have big soles—flat-bottomed tennies are best for feeling the board. If you just sunk all your money into your new skateboard and don't have the cash to splurge on new shoes, look in your closet for a pair of leather, flat-bottomed tennies. If you're planning to pull some aggro tricks that require jumping off your board, you may want to wear shoes with slightly more padding, such as sneakers made

>>> FIND IT NOW: Shoes

Circa
www.c1rca.com

DC Shoes
www.dcgirls.com

DVS
www.dvs-girls.com

Etnies
www.etniesgirl.com

Vans
www.vans.com

for basketball. Non-skid soles will help to grip the asphalt when you push the board. Flip-flops and other shoes will fly off when you're pushing or fall and leave your feet exposed to injury.

Clothes

The truth is you can really wear whatever you'd like. We leave the fashion choices entirely up to you. You can be a total girly-girl, go with a skater-chic vibe, or bust some look that no one has ever seen before—your call. But on the practical side, you need to make sure your clothes work appropriately with your safety gear. Wearing shorts and T-shirts is best for allowing knee and elbow pads to fit snugly against your skin. If you're wearing jeans, don't wear your pads under your pants (duh!). You'll certainly tear a hole and you won't be able to slide on the slick surface of the knee covering if you're on a ramp.

FIND IT NOW: Clothes <<<

All Girl Skate Jam
www.allgirlskatejam.com

Burly Girls
www.burlygirls.com

Nikita Clothing
www.nikitaclothing.com

Roxy
www.roxy.com

Sessions
www.sessions.com

Volcom
www.volcom.com

SAFETY EQUIPMENT

Safety rule #1: At the beginning, you need to wear all your safety gear. You can't get away with wearing some of these products—you need to wear them all properly. Plus, safety equipment is required at most skate parks and for lessons. Don't skimp on these items. Buy top of the line. After all, it's your body you're looking after and that's something you can't replace. Injury will only lead to less time on your board!

As you become a better skater, you'll be able to ditch the Michelin man look for a balance between safety and style. It's simply a matter of wearing the right amount of safety gear for what you're doing. When the best skater in the world is trying heavy tricks, she'll have on ALL her gear and no one will think she looks like a geek. Why? Because for her, pushing the envelope means falling, and if she falls she'd better have on her safety gear. Same goes for you. If you fall, you'd better be dressed for it. Right now, as you start learning, you could fall at any moment, so wear all your gear, all the time.

As you get better, you'll need less gear for basic riding. Some of your less critical stuff can stay at home during your ride to grab your mocha frap. That said, we're going to give you two additional bits of encouragement to wear safety gear: 1) Helmets save lives! Nothing more to say than that. 2) Don't forget to consider traffic. You might not have planned to perform crazy tricks on your ride to Starbucks, but things can turn ugly if some dumb driver cuts you off in an attempt to get his grande java two seconds sooner.

Helmets

Tired of hearing about helmets? Sorry, but they're *that* important. A helmet is a must for all skaters. It's the law in many states for riders under the age of 18 to wear a helmet when skateboarding. Made up of a high-density, impact-resistant ABS plastic outer shell and a shock absorbing, thick inner liner, helmets can protect you from a multitude of head injuries. The helmet you pur-

chase should offer full head coverage with extended rear coverage against backward falls. Make sure to get a skate-specific helmet. Others, such as bicycle helmets, may not offer protection for the back of your head. Make sure you get one that fits correctly, too; don't go borrowing your older sister's or friend's if it's too loose or too tight. It should fit snuggly over your head and strap under your chin (keep the chinstrap tight). Wearing a helmet without the chinstrap connected is like not wearing a helmet at all. Helmets range anywhere from $25 to $45. The good news is that skate manufactures are making cool-looking helmets these days, so you get to pick your favorite color and style. You can find quality helmets by Triple Eight, Nutcase, Bern and Pro-Tec, a favorite in the skating world.

Padding

Knee pads protect with hard outer shells and energy-absorbing foam padding. Elasticized straps hold the pads securely in place. Knee pads are a necessary accessory for both street and ramp skaters. Ramp skaters go to their knees when they fall, so knee pads are an absolute must. To make sure your knee pad is placed correctly, pull your foot back towards your butt so that your knee is pointing straight down. Make sure that the hard plate is directly over your kneecap. You can wear a neoprene knee gasket underneath your pad to keep it snug. The knee gaskets are also good if you're wearing pants and notice your pads keep slipping down. Wear the knee gasket under your pants and the knee pad over.

> **Tip:** The Bicycle Helmet <<< Safety Institute recommends making sure to buy a skateboard helmet that has either the ASTM F-1492 or Snell N-94 certification sticker inside.

Elbow pads have molded caps and lightweight pads to protect your elbows. To make sure your elbow pad is placed correctly, do the same as with your knee pads. Bend your arm so your elbow is facing straight out and make sure

the hard plate is directly over the pointy part of your elbow. Secure the Velcro straps tightly to ensure that the pad stays in place.

Wrist guards provide protection for wrists and palms. They should be light-weight and not restrict movement. Wrist guards take the impact in a fall instead of your wrist. Wrist guards should have a brace that goes around the wrist, with hard plastic that runs from the palm to below your wrist. Wrist braces are great, but you'll need to learn how to fall properly in order to get the best use out of them. Harbinger pads have great wrist guards designed to fit girls and women perfectly. Pro-Designed pads are plush with custom colors and designs such as cheetah-, zebra- and snake-skin patterns.

>>> FIND IT NOW: Gear

Bern
www.bernunlimited.com

Harbinger Skate
www.harbingerskate.com

Nutcase Helmets
www.nutcasehelmets.com

Pro-Tec
www.pro-tec.net

Pro-Designed
www.prodesigned.com

Triple Eight
www.triple8.com

Sunscreen

If you plan to skate outdoors for more than 20 minutes, you're going to need to wear sun-screen. Even if the day is cloudy or overcast, the sun's ultraviolet rays can travel through the clouds. Choose a broad-spectrum sunscreen (protects against both UVA and UVB rays) with an SPF of 15 or higher. You're going to need to apply your sunscreen 30 minutes before you head out the door so that it can adhere to your skin. Make sure to hit all the areas your clothes don't cover, such as your face, ears and the backs of your hands and neck. If you sweat a lot (and you probably will when skateboarding), purchase a water-resistant formula.

> **Hint:** Make sure to stop and adjust all your equipment frequently when you ride. How lame would it be to get an injury even though you were wearing your pads but they were out of place? <<<

ALL DRESSED UP BUT WHERE TO GO?

Now that you've got all your gear, it's time to start your skateboarding career. There are several different styles of skateboarding you can check out. For those of you dying to get started, grab a friend and head outside. The best place to begin is at a park with smooth concrete surfaces or the sidewalk or cul-de-sac in your neighborhood. However, we've said it before, we'll say it again now, and we'll say it 100 more times: Be wary of cars, buses and any other metal objects hurtling towards you at Mach 3. Don't go shooting out of your driveway into the street. Make sure you're not skating in your driveway at 6 o'clock, when your dad usually pulls in. Have a reliable friend on the lookout. Be safe!

Skateboarding Is Not a Crime!

(But we wouldn't want you to get arrested.) For your own sake, never skate on a busy street. Period, end of sentence. Even if it's allowed, don't do it—it is just too dangerous. On the other hand, there are lots of great, safe skate spots that are off-limits. Arrgh! You can absolutely be arrested for skating somewhere that has a "no trespassing" or "no skateboarding" sign. These spots may look tempting, but it'll never be worth the hassle of getting a ticket or arrested. Make sure to check out the skateboarding laws in your area. Many large cities don't allow you to skate on the sidewalk at all. A big concern of "the man" is that skateboarding destroys property. Now, who's to say if it really does or not (more than normal wear and tear), but be considerate. Don't perform any tricks or jumps on unstable or fragile surfaces (for your benefit as well as others).

Another way some newbies choose to learn is by heading to a skate park. Skate parks are a great choice because they have smooth surfaces and transitions made especially for skateboarding, and you don't need to worry about cars. Some may have equipment for street skating, half-pipes, bowls or a combination of all. If you want to go to a skate park right away, it would be in your best interest (and in the best interest of everyone around you, too!) to take a lesson, or to go when it's less crowded.

Don't forget your helmet (many of the parks require elbow and knee pads, too, so call ahead to find out the rules). Most parks will run you between $4 to $15 per session or day, although some city parks are free. Check out these websites for a list of skate parks around the world, or surf the web for "skate park + your city" to find one in your area.

Street Skating

Street skating is just what it sounds like—skating on the street, sidewalk or any open asphalt area. To street skate is to touch the soul of skating. There's a freedom to street skating because you're not bound by any walls. Before skate parks became common, skaters used the urban terrain for tricks on banks, jumps, curbs, gaps, hand rails and stairs. The bad part of street skating is the possibility of being told you can't skate somewhere or getting kicked out. Remember: It's illegal to trespass, even if a place looks like it would be a brilliant street-skating area. Skate parks often have specific areas for street skaters to practice their tricks and this could be a safer, more legal alternative.

Vert

Vert, meaning vertical, skating is performed in a half-pipe or bowl. Vert skating began in the empty swimming pools around the country. Kids found a surface that went completely perpendicular to the ground, allowing them to ride up and even out of the pool. This is called an "aerial" or getting "air." Getting air became so exciting to skaters that they began to build ramps shaped like a "U." These half-pipes allow riders to skate back and forth, building speed and eventually coming completely out and getting air before landing. The half-pipe has a vertical wall, a flat bottom, and a curved section, called a transition or "tranny," that takes you from the flat to the vertical. The top part of the wall is called the edge or coping. Skaters can perform tricks on the coping or even bypass it completely, doing tricks in the air.

Slalom and Downhill

Slalom and downhill skateboarding share some characteristics such as speed and hills, but they are two very different animals. Downhill has long been a popular form of skating. Mostly it involves heading down a steep hill as fast as possible. Downhill is about raw speed.

Riders feel more freedom than slalom, as the only boundaries are the edges of the pavement. Downhill racers need a high level of confidence as they reach high speeds on mountain roads. Their races involve two to four racers on the same course at the same time.

In slalom skating, skaters haul down a designated course as fast as possible. This was popular in the 1960s and '70s, and is seriously making a comeback. Slalom is the art of seeing a course of cones and picking the fastest line through it. Racing demands concentration, quick motion, core strength, and a skateboard with narrow, loose trucks. Slalom is a very technically advanced sport, and if you go to a race, you will see many different types of boards and trucks.

Skater Aid

Lessons, either through skate parks, skate camps or private instructors, are available to skaters of all ages. Check online or with your local skate park or skate shop for lessons in your area. A typical lesson may last an hour (anything longer and your concentration may wane or you could fatigue, leading to injury) and cost anywhere from $20 to $70; there also may be an additional charge for insurance. The lesson will most likely cover safety (including how to properly wear your protective equipment), stance, movement and coordination (how to push your board and lean into turns). You'll also learn how to start and, more importantly, how to stop.

>>> FIND IT NOW: Parks

www.skateboardparks.com

www.skateboardpark.com

www.skateboarding.com/
skate/skateparks

Group lessons are great in that you can feed off of one another's energy and encourage each other. However, it's not a bad idea for the brand spankin' new skateboarder to take a private lesson. Once you learn the basics, you'll be better equipped to participate in a group lesson. Private lessons go over the same skills as the group lesson but you can move at your own pace and have someone right there to watch over you. Or you could spend a week or more learning and perfecting your sick skater moves at summer camp, an excellent way to get a big dose of skating all at once with many other amped skaters.

First things first: Before you even show up to your lesson, the school or instructor should ask your age, ability level, and what style of skater you are (or are hoping to become). Make sure they take an interest in you. If they're like, "Yeah, just come on down," you may want to find a more professional group, someone who takes teaching seriously. Make sure your instructor or the skate park staff is trained in first aid and CPR. Most of the time, you'll need to bring your own equipment. Helmets are required at almost all parks, and some also insist on knee pads, elbow pads and wrist guards, so check ahead. The instructor can tell you where to purchase gear if you haven't already.

FIND IT NOW: All-Girl Lessons/Camps <<<

All Girl Skate Jam
www.allgirlskatejam.com

Boardfest
www.boardfest.com

Etnies Girls Get on Board
www.etniesgirl.com

Girlie Camps
www.girliecamps.com

OP Girls Learn to Ride
www.girlslearntoride.com

Here is a list of skate camps across the United States:

California

Magdalena Ecke YMCA, Encinitas
http://ecke.ymca.org

Mission Valley YMCA, San Diego
www.ymca.org/missionvalley

Northridge Skate Park, Northridge
www.northridgeskatepark.com

Point X Camp, Aguanga
www.pointx.com

Skatelab Skateboarding Camp, Simi Valley
www.skatelab.com

Southern California School of Skateboarding, Venice
www.skateboardlessons.com

Strawberry Canyon Youth Sports, Berkeley
www.oski.org

Visalia YMCA, Visalia
www.skatecamp.org

Woodward Camp, Tehachapi
www.campwoodward.com

Florida
Skatelab Skateboarding Camp, Atlantic Beach
www.skatelab.com

New Hampshire
Rye Airfield Charlie Wilkins RAMP CAMP, Rye
www.ryeairfield.com

Waterville Valley Skate Camp, Waterville Valley
www.waterville.com/summer/skatecamp.html

Oregon
High Cascade Skateboard Camp, Mt. Hood
www.highcascade.com

Pennsylvania
Woodward Camp, Woodward
www.campwoodward.com

Texas
Eisenberg's Summer Camp, Plano
www.eisenbergs.com/camphuh.html

Washington
Island Lake Camp, Poulsbo
www.cristacamps.com

Wisconsin
Woodward Camp: Cable
www.campwoodward.com

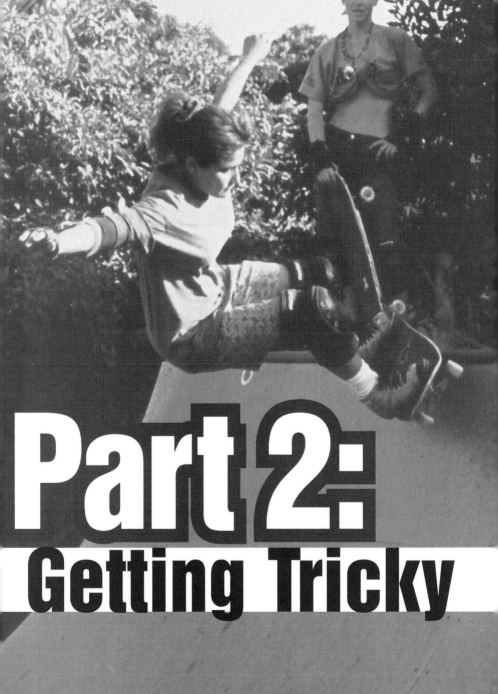

Part 2:
Getting Tricky

Chapter 4:
Let's Go Skate:
The Basics

So you're all set with your board and protective equipment. Now you'll need to find a nice quiet place where there's no traffic to practice. An empty playground, a school parking lot on the weekend, an unused basketball court or even a quiet neighborhood sidewalk will do—smooth surfaces are always the safest.

IN THE BEGINNING

Bring your board over to the grass. Stand up on your board. Which foot do you put forward? It doesn't matter which foot you choose; it's totally your choice. However, riding with your left foot forward is called regular stance. If you decide to ride with your right foot in front, this is called "goofy-footed."

If you aren't sure which is your forward foot, try this: Step on the skateboard as if you were going to skate away. Your natural reaction to the placement of your feet on the board will pretty much determine what your stance will be from here on out when you skate. Or try this fun test. Take off your sneakers and slide across the kitchen floor in your socks. Which foot do you put in

front? If you're still unsure, try to skate both ways and eventually you'll discover what's right for you.

Stand on your board sideways with your front foot resting over the front trucks and your back foot on the tail. See the bolts on the top of your board? Put your front foot right on top of them. Your feet will be perpendicular with the board, meaning your heels will be close to one edge of the board and the toes close to the opposite edge of the board.

Keep your knees bent and your body loose so that you can absorb any bumps. Your knees will act as shock absorbers. Keep your body centered over the board; try not to stick your butt out because this will throw you off balance. Keep your center low. Don't forget to use your arms to help keep you balanced.

Try rocking your weight from your heels to your toes. Feel the deck of your skateboard move under your feet. This is how you're going to turn once you're out there riding.

GET MOVING

Once you feel confident standing on your board, you're ready to roll.

1 Slide your back foot onto the kicktail (the back of the board that turns up at an angle) and press down with your back foot harder than you are pressing down with your front foot. Press until your front wheels lift just off the grass. Remember that if you press down too hard with your back leg, you'll pop one mega-wheelie but also lose your balance and go flying off your board. The key is to keep control and balance by keeping

Wheelies

Rating: 🛹

With skateboarding, wheelies are not about showing off or just used in tricks—they're an important skill used in everyday riding, such as turning and stopping. So before you get off the grass, learn how to balance and control your board while doing a wheelie.

your weight on both feet, but to press a little harder with your back foot. When you put your weight on your back foot and lift up the nose, your body will have to adjust slightly, hip out and shoulders forward, to maintain your center of balance. Try raising the nose higher and higher, while staying balanced and in control, until the tail of the board touches the ground.

3

4

2-4 Next, learn to move the nose of the board from side to side. Pop a low wheelie and rotate your body forward or back so the board's nose actually moves in the same direction. Lift the nose and shift forward, then place the wheels back on the ground. Your front foot should now be in front of your back foot. Lift the nose and shift the nose of the board back so that your front foot is behind your back foot.

> Wheelies are only done on boards that have a kicktail. Don't try wheelies on a flat longboard or cruiser that doesn't turn up at the tail. If your longboard only has a kicktail in the back, you can practice lifting the nose only. <<<

Take your board for a walk. After mastering front wheelies, try putting your front foot on the nose and push down so that you do a back wheelie by lifting your back wheels. Then try "walking" your board forward and backward by shifting the nose forward then changing your weight to the front foot and shifting the tail forward. Now try going backward. This helps you learn weight control and balance and will prepare you for future tricks.

It's important to practice pushing before you even start rolling. So when you're still on the grass, try this:

Pushing

Rating: 🛹

To get your board rolling, you'll push with your back foot. Doing this involves stepping on and off the board with your back foot and rotating your front foot in a fashion similar to a dance move.

1 Stand with both feet sideways on your board so that your front foot is over the bolts and your back foot is near the tail.

2 Keeping your front foot over the bolts, step onto the grass with your back foot. Simultaneously rotate your body so that you're facing forward. While you rotate your body, turn both feet so that they're facing forward, parallel with your board. Your front foot should still be centered over the front bolts, but now your toes are toward the nose, and the heel is toward the tail; your back foot is on the grass and parallel to the board.

3 Now bring your back foot back onto the board while rotating your body so you're facing sideways. Your feet will be over the bolts and perpendicular again. If you keep the weight on the ball of your front foot, it'll be easier to rotate. Practice this until it feels natural and you can do it without looking at your feet. Once you're moving, you'll need to keep your eyes on where you're going. Looking at your feet while pushing your board is a sure-fire way to motor right into something nasty in your path, like a hole, rock or person walking right in front of you.

1 2 3

The first way to stop your board may sound stupid, but remember, it's just for your first couple of tries. Just stand on the board til you stop (aka, Basic Stopping 0). How stupid is that? On your first couple of times rolling forward, pick a spot that's long and straight and push only once, letting yourself slowly roll to a stop. You'll be going so slow that you'll stop without doing anything. It's all part of learning. But that's the idea, isn't it?

Basic Stopping 1—Step Off/Run Out: The most natural (but maybe not the safest) way to stop is to simply step off your board. When you're still learning and traveling at slow speeds, this move is

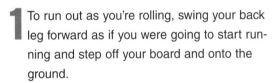
Stopping

Rating:

Before you get off the grass and start rolling, you need to have a better plan for stopping other than crashing into something. In case you hadn't noticed, there are no brakes on a skateboard. In a second, you'll see that sometimes crashing is not just the only way to stop, but it's often the best way. However, until you're ready for that, you should learn safer ways to stop.

fine, but as soon as you build speed or get on a ramp, this can be dangerous.

1 To run out as you're rolling, swing your back leg forward as if you were going to start running and step off your board and onto the ground.

2 With the foot that was your front foot on the board, kick your skateboard backward, away from you. You should come off your board at a slight run since you're trying to continue that same momentum you had while riding. Again, this move can turn ugly if you have too much speed because you won't be able to run out fast enough and you'll be sure to hit the ground. Make sure to be aware of where your board goes once you step off.

Basic Stopping 2—Foot Dragging:

As you gain speed and balance, slow yourself down or come to a stop by dragging the sole of your back foot along the ground. This is similar to pushing in that your front foot will be facing forward, centered over the bolts, and your back foot will be off the board and on the ground. But instead of pushing off with your back foot, it'll be against the ground, creating friction to slow you down. Some people choose to drag the toe of their shoe along the ground to prevent wearing their shoes out unevenly.

Basic Stopping 3—Tail Dragging:

A more advanced way to stop is the "skid your tail" trick. Think of this as a "wheelie" stop. So if you skipped practicing the wheelies on the grass, go back and give it a try. I know you want to get moving—and you're almost there—but wheelies are a great way to stop and good practice for balance as well.

To skid your tail, push down on the tail of your board while you're rolling until it connects with the sidewalk. This will create friction between the tail of your board and the cement and bring you to a stop. The downside is that over time this trick will wear out the tail of your board. Save this trick until your balance on your board is perfected, since lifting the nose while riding may send you flying off your board and onto your butt.

ROLLING ALONG

Remember that skateboards love the earth, are good for the environment and don't burn gas. To motor your board, you simply push with your back foot. Pushing is what you'll do to roll your board over a flat or uphill surface (the board will roll downhill on its own).

I know you're thinking enough is enough—I want to get skating. If you've read and practiced the stuff we just told you about, then you're ready to head over to a flat patch of sidewalk and actually skate. If you haven't and instead you skipped to right here, girl, are you in for a big surprise called "soft skin meets hard cement"!)

> Very few people use their **<<<** front foot to push (which is called "mongo"), but if that's more comfortable for you, that's fine.

Once you've found an empty, smooth, flat surface, you're ready to start rolling. Start with your front foot on the board, over your front truck and facing forward, and your back foot on the sidewalk. With your back foot, push off the cement so that your board is rolling, then place your back foot back on the tail of the board, both feet sideways, but keep your head facing forward. Always look at where you're going and not at your feet. Roll to a stop.

Start again, but this time as you slow down, rotate your front foot to parallel with the board, take your back foot off the board and push again. Keep practicing until you're comfortable keeping the board moving while taking your back foot off and back on the board.

Remember that on your first couple of pushes forward, you should just roll to a stop, but after that you should be practicing your basic stops. Don't continue pushing your board to get mad speed when you still haven't practiced a stop at slow speeds. What you should do is practice moving with a couple of pushes then stepping off to stop.

Continue running out at higher and higher speeds so that you can safely go faster and faster. Now try a toe drag, or if you're feeling really confident, a tail slide. Sweet!

Moving & Stopping

Rating: $

Most skaters will push more than once to gain speed, about three to four times before they return their back foot to the board. But because speed isn't your friend just yet, push only once right now. Remember that you shouldn't go as fast as possible, but only as fast as you're able to stop or run out. Going faster than your stopping ability means you're out of control and present a danger to yourself and anyone who steps out in front of you.

If you have small wheels and loose-set trucks, you'll get sharper but more squirrely turns. Big wheels and tight trucks will give you more stability, and you'll take bigger, more arcing turns. Here you'll learn how to control your weight to start and end a turn. At the beginning, you'll need a lot of room. An empty parking lot or playground is a great place to start turning.

Turning

Rating: ▯

Once you get rolling, you're going to want to learn how to turn your board. Your wheels and trucks on your skateboard do most of the turning for you. Your set-up will determine how quickly your board can turn.

Carving: The term "carving" comes from surfing, where a rider makes slow arcing turns up and down the face of the wave. Carving in skateboarding is similar in that you'll be making wide, loose turns on cement.

1 Push yourself so you're rolling forward. Turn your head and shoulders in the direction you want to go and the rest of your body will follow. To turn "toeside," put a little more weight on your toes than your heels. Keep your knees bent and body loose. Try it again by looking over your shoulder and putting some weight on your heels. Now you're turning "heelside."

2 Once you feel comfortable shifting your weight, you can connect your turns. Push down on your toes, then straighten back up and put weight on your heels. Stay calm and focused, and keep the motions smooth. Don't forget to look in the direction you're turning. By facing one way, your body will follow. You should have just made an S-turn. Wahoo!

The more weight on your heels or toes, the sharper your turn. Experiment making soft, loose turns, then tighter, sharper turns—big S's and little S's.

Tick-Tacking: Instead of turning by carving, you can tick-tack. Think of tick-tacking as turning while popping a wheelie. You did a little bit of this on the grass earlier but, not surprisingly, you'll find that it's a bit trickier while in motion.

1 To tick-tack, push on the kicktail to lift the nose of your board off the ground just a little bit.

2 Now while the board is in a low wheelie, shift the weight on your front foot to the right so that the nose of the board moves to the right. This is similar to carving "toeside." The key to tick-tacking is getting your forward foot to do two things at the same time: keep in check how high the nose lifts and also move the nose to the side.

To release from the tick-tack position, put your weight back over the nose. Next, try shifting the nose of the board back for a tick-tack turn that's like a "heelside" turn.

Kick Turn:

Kick Turn: Take a tick-tack, make it massive, and you have a kick turn. This turn takes your board halfway around while the nose is in the air.

1 To do this, put your weight on the back foot, lift up the front wheels.

2-3 Turn 180 degrees and head back the way you came. Sounds crazy, but it works. Start doing kick turns when you're still. Try going halfway around, then see if you spin all the way around and end up where you started for a full 360 degrees.

As you get more secure on your board, try kick turns when you're rolling slowly. You can do this on the street or the ramp. Pros do kick turns on the half-pipe as they build speed.

Intermediate Stopping 1—Slide:
A brake slide is when you're skating and you slide out the back wheels of your board so that your board turns 90 degrees, creating a skidding effect. You'll end up facing slightly sideways to the direction in which you were headed. (If you've ever snowboarded, it's a similar motion to stopping on a hill.)

1-2 Put a lot of pressure down on that back foot and, with a quick, jerky motion, shove the back of the board sideways. Remember to stay low, and keep your hands out for balance. Does this sound a little scary? It's a more advanced maneuver, so hold off using this form of stopping until you're really secure on your board.

More Stopping

Rating: 𝟏.

Once you've mastered basic stopping (pages 45–46), you're ready to try these more advanced ways to stop. You'll see that one of them involves literally falling off your board, or bailing. (Don't try to explain this idea to your mom—she won't get it.)

Intermediate Stopping

2—Bail Queen: Bailing is actually more complicated than it sounds. The bad news? You can't practice tricks without bailing. The good news? The only way you'll get better is by falling. Even pros bail all the time. Watch them on a vert ramp as they bail on almost every run. Pro skaters are pro fallers, and to skateboard, you need to learn to fall with the best of them.

If you're street skating or riding a small ramp where you're close to the flat bottom, you can run off your board. While stepping off sounds easy, you need to make sure you come off your board at a run in order to travel with the same momentum as you were skating. If you have a lot of speed going, it's actually better to fall. Yes, we said it: It's better to fall!

When falling, try to tuck into a ball and allow yourself to roll however you can. This will displace the impact. You can also use your pads to land. But whatever you do, keep in mind that the safest way to be in a fall is fluid, limber and calm. With falling, if you don't panic and overreact, you'll probably be all right. So stay relaxed and ready to react. Then just fall and roll.

With all this talk of falling, don't forget to wear your helmet, knee, and elbow and wrist pads. Now you truly are a bail queen!

What Not to Do

Whatever you do, try not to land on your board—ouch! If you can, try to push it away from you during a fall.

Avoid putting out your hands when you fall, even though your natural reaction is to do just that. You're likely to twist, bruise or break a wrist or even an arm by doing so. Even if you're wearing wrist guards, which will reduce the chance of injury, this is a bad habit.

Intermediate Stopping 3—Knee Slides: You're probably

thinking, "I'm getting good at riding and stopping on a flat surface, so now I want to try going vert." Once again, you need to learn how to stop before you get started (unless you figure out a way to read this section of the book while in the middle of your ride). Bailing in a half-pipe or pool is a little different than bailing on flat ground. You need to get to the bottom of the ramp the safest way possible because gravity is going to take you there no matter what. To do this, you'll need to fall to your knees and slide down. This is truly the most natural and practical way to bail your trick or stop. Before you even bring your board onto the ramp with you, you'll need to learn how to fall to your knees. You might feel lame practicing this, but this is a must-do.

1 To practice falling to your knees, first put on your pads and helmet—especially your knee pads with plastic caps (duh). Next, run up the transition or the side of the ramp.

2-3 Turn your body so you're facing back down, and then go to your knees by bending your legs under you (like you're sitting on your feet), falling onto your knees, shins and tops of feet. Keep your upper body upright as you slide down. Practice this a couple of times until it feels instinctual. Now you're ready to grab your board.

Starting Off: To start skating on a half-pipe or in a pool, begin at the bottom and simply push yourself up one side and let yourself roll back down and then roll right back up the other side. Your body will be facing in one direction so when you come back down and up the other side, you'll be riding "fakie" (your back foot is now your front foot). Just pushing once from the bottom isn't going to get you very far because you'll quickly slow to a stop at the bottom.

To keep going and get higher, you need to compress and pump your legs, just like you build speed on a swing by pumping your legs back and forth. If you didn't do this, you wouldn't gain any momentum and would just stall out.

Half-Pipes
Rating: 🛹🛹

Half-pipes are U-shaped ramps usually made of wood. Anything shorter than eight feet high is called a mini-ramp, which you'll find at most skate parks. Vert ramps are another kind of half-pipe, running 10 to 13 feet high. Mini-ramps can be less intimidating than vert ramps so start here. Don't try to do a black-diamond ski run before you've gone down the bunny slope, get it?

1 Start with a push on the flat bottom. As you head up one side, you'll want to compress by bending your knees. You'll feel yourself peak—which is the final moment before you go back down.

2 When you start back down, pump by straightening you legs, pressing your weight down onto the board. As you go up the other side of the half-pipe,

compress again by bending your knees, feel the peak and then pump as you come back down. Compress on your way back up, feel the peak, decompress on the way down. Compress. Peak. Pump. Compress. Peak. Pump. All the while, the higher and higher you go.

>>> The expressions "backside" and "frontside" originated in surfing. "Frontside" is when your body faces the wave. So if you have your left foot forward (regular stance) and are heading down a wave to the right, you'd be traveling frontside; if you went left, you'd be backside, with your back facing the wave. It's the same in skating. Imagine that the half-pipe is a wave, so if you're facing the vertical section, you're frontside; if your back is to it, you're going backside.

In the beginning, touch the nose of your board when you peak and the tail of your board when you peak riding fakie. This will get you into a low position—knees bent, arms out. Also, the higher you look up the ramp, the higher you'll go.

Keep practicing until you get comfortable going higher and higher up the transition. Also, keep practicing your knee slides as you get higher and higher. The girl who finds herself bailing off her board while eight feet up the side of a ramp better not be the same girl who has never done a knee slide from more than three feet, or she won't be a very happy girl when what goes up comes down—hard.

Dropping In: Once you can get your board all the way up to the coping (the edge of the half-pipe), you can start to think about dropping in.

1 Start at the top. Place the tail of your board onto the lip with your back foot on the tail. When you're ready, place your front foot over the front bolts. You'll be balancing in a wheelie over the edge of the half-pipe. ("Way to go, baby, you've come a long way from those wheelies in the grass!")

2-3 Finally, shift your weight onto your front foot and drop in. You have to lean forward, staying compressed with your hands out for balance and control, or you'll do a "Mr. Wilson" (when you drop in and the majority of your weight is toward the back of the board, creating a wheelie effect that causes your feet to slip out and you to land on your back). When first learning how to drop in, you must exaggerate leaning forward or you'll eat it! A good tip is to pretend you're touching the nose of your board as you drop in. This will keep you leaning forward. You'll probably bail on the first couple of tries. If you do, remember to slide to your knees or tuck and roll.

Before You Get on the Board

If you know how to do an ollie (page 66), you can jump up onto whatever edge you want to slide along. But if you haven't perfected your ollie just yet, you can practice on a curb that connects to a driveway since you can roll right onto the curb edge without having to ollie onto the curb.

Now Do It

1 Ride in the gutter toward the driveway.

2 As you cross the driveway, maneuver the wheels on one side of your board into the driveway while the other wheels remain in the gutter. When you get to the other side of the driveway, you'll ride right up onto the curb.

3 As you hit the rise in the curb, make sure that you're balanced. It's also very important that you bend your knees slightly.

Intro 50-50

Rating: 🛹🛹

This is the fun skating maneuver where you slide (or "grind") along a rail, curb, coping or some type of edge on your trucks instead of rolling along a surface on your wheels. This will take some getting used to since, as you grind along the edge, you'll be balancing the board, pressing firm on your trucks while using your heels and toes, instead of having the four wheels to keep you balanced.

Apryl Woodcock does a 5-0 grind.

If you do start sliding, the wheels that were in the gutter will be in mid-air and thus drop down. This will start to flip the board and pull the other wheels off the sidewalk and into the air. You want to get your balance just right, sliding on the edge with none of the wheels touching the ground. If you press too hard in either direction, you'll flip into the gutter or get tossed onto the sidewalk. That's why it's important to have your knees bent and to be light on your board. Press down on the sidewalk side so that the board remains stable and under your feet. Your momentum will keep you moving forward in this balanced position as you slide along the edge of the curb. Now you're grinding.

Before your momentum stops, slowly begin to lean your weight inward toward the street. All in one motion, scoot your back wheels toward the ground, followed by your front wheels, and ride away.

Other Cool Moves

As you improve, you might want to try a *5-0 grind*, when you grind on the rear truck only. This requires a lot of balance. Definitely a more advanced trick. Cara-Beth Burnside always seems to pull these out so smoothly from her bag of tricks.

Don't forget: When first thinking about grinding a curb, <<< check how slippery it is. A painted curb will be more slippery (which you don't want when you're first starting out), and often curbs are painted red on that edge where they meet a driveway. Or if you're in an area where a lot of skater hang out, you should do a wax check to see if other skaters have been waxing up the curb. Skaters may wax a curb with skate wax to lessen the friction for rail grinds. If they have, it may be super slippery. Waxing a curb is a good thing as you get better because it'll only make your grind lengthier and louder. Sweet!

Bonus: Cool Trick

Skating well and practicing hard are the best ways to be cool. But in the meantime, one way to look like a true skater girl is by being able to kick your board up into your hand. You've probably seen skaters do this at the end of a ride or when they're done riding and heading indoors. Again, this is a good one to try on the grass if you need a little more control of your board.

1-2 When you're off your board, step down hard on the tail and try to grab the nose of the skateboard in your hand. Give it a whirl. It seems like it would be easy, but it takes a little practice. So we recommend trying it a couple of times before you head to the skate park, step on the kicktail and give yourself a bloody nose. So not cool!

Chapter 5:
Other Tricks

This chapter introduces more advanced skate tricks. There are literally hundreds of tricks to work on. You can spend your whole life either learning new tricks or inventing some of your own. That's the beauty of skateboarding—it never gets boring. The tricks listed in this chapter are all keystones to build on.

Be patient, just like at the beginning. These tricks will take time to perfect. We don't want you to get hurt, so before taking these on, make sure you have mastered the basics from the previous chapters. Even at this stage, it's not a bad idea to take a lesson or head to a skate camp for some quality instruction and skate time.

Do It

You'll most likely start with a backside kick turn, which means you'll turn toward your toes. (Sounds like it should be the opposite, doesn't it? But because "backside" means having your back to the obstacle, you'll be turning away from the wall of the ramp.)

Start low on the ramp. As you ride up, bend your knees and stay as low as you can to your board. Because you're now up on the transition, balance comes even more into play. As you peak, press back on the tail and rotate your board so that it's facing back down the ramp. Keep trying to take your kick turn higher and higher up the ramp.

As you improve, try rotating frontside—turning toward your heels (as shown).

Kick Turn

Rating: 🛹🛹

Once you've mastered your kick turn (see Chapter 4) on the street, it's time to take it to the ramp or any place with a transition (aka "tranny"). A wooden ramp is more forgiving than cement and may be a good place to start. When you're faking (that is, "pumping" back and forth on the ramp), as you roll up toward the coping, start rotating your upper body while looking over your shoulder at the same time. Your board will follow the rest of your body as it turns 180 degrees. When you skate down the ramp, you'll be facing the opposite direction from which you were originally skating.

BONUS: COOL TRICK

Here is another all-time "wow, that looks so cool" trick that actually isn't very hard. At the bottom of a ramp or pool, hold onto the tail of your board. Run up the transition until you're near the coping. Just before you get there, while you're still holding onto the tail, jump on your board with both feet and roll down. It may sound complicated, but if you can do the last bit all in one motion, you've got it down. This one takes a little practice but isn't that hard—and it looks super sick! This is Cara-Beth's classic way of getting back on her board every time.

Before You Get on the Board

To do a backside grind, you need to be able to get yourself up to the lip, or coping, of the ramp.

Now Do It

1 Roll up toward the lip.

Backside Grind

Rating: ▌▌▪

The backside grind is one of the first vert tricks you'll learn. For those of you who are a little more cautious: Once you can grind the coping on a ramp, you're ready to drop in.

2-3 Once you're up, turn your body so that it's facing back down into the transition, and let your back truck grind (that is, slide across) the coping. Put pressure on your back truck so that it slides hard and makes that oh-so-awesome sound—a grind!—before dropping back in.

Other Moves

Once you can perform a grind, you can also practice a *50-50 grind* (see photo above), which is where you slide on both trucks, or an *axle stall* (rating: 3). For an axle stall, come up to the coping and, all in one motion, place your back trucks down, followed by your front trucks. Pause for a moment, then drop back in.

Now you can begin to try to turn frontside on a ramp, where your front faces the coping and your back is to the flat bottom of the ramp. Before you know it, you'll be grinding backside and frontside. It's important that you try turning both ways right from the start so that you don't get used to turning only one way.

Before You Get on the Board

Try this first: Bend your knees, jump off just your back foot, bring your feet together in the air and land on both feet at the same time. Yes, it's a one-legged jump! This is like performing an ollie on the board.

Now Do It

1 OK, now onto your board for real ollies. Stand with your back foot on the tail of your board and your front foot in the middle of your board.

2-3 Bend your knees really, really far, then start to straighten your back leg really fast so that you pop down on the tail of your board and make it smack the ground. The harder you pop the tail, the higher you'll go.

Ollie

Rating: ▮▮▮

The ollie is at the essence of nearly all skateboard tricks. Any trick where a street skater gets air begins with an ollie. An ollie is done in one smooth motion of popping (stepping hard on) your tail and rolling your front foot forward to the nose as the back of the board follows the tip upward, off the ground. End result: The board has magically leapt into the air with all four wheels off the ground and the deck flat under your feet. Just like that, you're standing on your board in mid-air like Aladdin on his flying carpet.

4-5 Of course, with the tail going down to the ground, the nose of your board will fly up. This is just what you want. So as your back foot goes down, lift your front foot and let it fly up (but keep guiding it) into the air along with the nose of the board; keep the board in control by sliding your front foot up toward the nose of your board. You can't have your front foot flat against the board as you slide it since that will prevent the board from coming up. You should turn your ankle slightly so the outer edge of your shoe is the only part touching the board as it slides along. What you've done is lifted the board with your back foot and leveled it out in mid-air with your front foot.

Now, at the very moment that the tail smacks the ground and the board wants to fly upward, jump off your back leg. By jumping, you'll take your weight off the board so it can go skyward. Kick your front foot toward the nose, rolling your foot to scrape the grip tape with your pinky toe.

6 To land, flatten your front foot back on the board along with your back foot, just as you practiced on stable ground. Make sure to bend your legs as you touch the ground; this helps absorb the impact to your knees and ankles.

The important thing to remember is that timing is key. It'll take a while to master this trick but once you do, you'll have the skills to learn hundreds more.

Before You Get on the Board

To do a fakie rock, you need to be able to come up all the way to the lip of a ramp.

Fakie Rock

Rating: ▮▮▮▯

A fakie rock is when your front wheels come out of the half-pipe, you teeter-totter on your deck and then drop back in riding backwards.

Now Do It

1-2 Once you're at the top, let your front wheels roll over the coping so that half of your board is on the deck of the ramp. Then push your front foot down so that you rock forward with your deck against the coping as if you were going to have your front wheels just kiss the tabletop.

3-4 Now push back down on your back foot, just enough that you don't lock up your front trucks on the coping (this is the hard part), and drop back into the ramp backward. Keep your upper body back, especially when you slap the deck halfway over the coping, and just use your legs to rock your board.

Other Moves

Once you can do a fakie rock, you can try a regular *rock-n-roll* (see photo above). Ride up the tranny and slap your board on the platform. Make sure the front of your back trucks are touching the coping for better stability, balance at the peak for a few seconds, and then turn your body (like you would in a kick turn) 180 degrees back into the ramp and ride down the transition.

Before You Get on the Board

To do an acid drop, you need to have confidence as well as be able to keep your knees bent and look where you're planning to land.

Now Do It

1-2 Start off of a low curb. Ride right off it.

3 As you land on all four wheels, bend your knees and use them to absorb the shock. You'll need to keep your body relaxed and loose to land an acid drop without jamming your knees, ankles or back.

Acid Drop

Rating: 🛹🛹🛹🛹

An acid drop is where you skate straight off of something and freefall to the ground, flat bottom or, for your ankle's sake, hopefully a tranny, and land on all four wheels at the same time. Duane Peters, a 1970s skate punk legend, is credited with inventing acid drops.

1

2

3

Before You Get on the Board

You need to know how to do an ollie (page 66).

Now Do It

1 Pop a hefty ollie—the more air time you have, the more time you'll have to flip your board.

2 As you roll your front ankle up your grip tape, trying to place the side of your ankle on the board, flick the heel side of your skateboard, setting the board into a sideways flip. You need to take your back foot off your deck in order for the deck to flip.

Kickflip

Rating: 🛹🛹🛹🛹

The kickflip allows your board to, well, flip 360 degrees while you're over your board in mid-air. Pro-skateboarder Rodney Mullen is often credited with inventing and perfecting this trick.

3-4 Stay above your board while it's flipping and land with your back foot first to stop the board from flipping again (unless you're already moving on to a double kickflip!). Don't forget to crouch low on your landing to absorb the flat ground. While you don't use your hands to flip the board manually, you'll need to keep your arms and hands out by your side for balance.

While being interviewed at the <<< 2004 AGSJ in Hawaii, Elissa Steamer (X-Games Street gold medalist) was asked what her favorite trick was. Her response: a kickflip!

Before You Get on the Board

There are a few things you need to do before you even start your downhill career. First and foremost, make sure you're comfortable with turning, stopping and falling. You'll need a board with soft wheels; don't try to carve on hard wheels or your board will slide out from under you during your turns.

You must also master foot-breaking before getting more speed than you can safely run out. If you start to downhill slide, you must first practice sliding with your hands and knees on the board. Never ride without protection, especially knee pads and slide gloves, when working on your downhill skating. Practice sliding on your pads so that when you need them, falling

Downhill

Rating: ♦♦♦♦♦

Our friend, pro skater Isabelle Caudle calls downhill and carving the "grassroots of skating— you ride as though you're on a wave, carefree, silky and smooth." Sounds fun, right? Because you can pick up speed fast while traveling downhill, we list this trick as more advanced. As soon as you're even at a slight slope, gravity will start to pull and speed you up.

onto them properly will be instinctive. You'll have no time to think, so developing instinct through practice is paramount.

Now Do It

1 Start on a slightly sloped, traffic-free path with plenty of room to carve the large turns needed to keep your speed under control. Even if you're progressing well with your skating, start on smaller hills before you move to something bigger. Stand with your feet shoulder-width apart. If you're on a longer board, make sure your foot isn't too far back from your front truck (this could cause you to lose control of the board, possibly get speed wobbles and then get pitched).

2 Start by cutting across the hill at an angle and then back again, making loose "S" turns. Travel from curb to curb until this motion begins to feel fluid. Make sure to keep your speed under control, allowing you to run out if necessary. Also make sure your body is facing downhill at all times, even when you're turning. This will help control your speed and keep the ride from becoming too steep. Soon you'll become a downhill diva!

1

2a

2b

Before You Get on the Board

You'll need full protective equipment and slide gloves, which will protect your hands. Slide gloves are usually made of leather and have replaceable hard plastic palms for sliding. Begin on hard wheels, which will slide much more easily ("break loose") than soft wheels. As your sliding improves, you can change to softer wheels, combining a smooth downhill ride with controlled power slides.

Now Do It

Practice getting really low on your board while you're skating. Bend your knees, tucking your rear knee to the deck near your front foot to come into a full squat. Once you can do that, head over to a wide but shallow hill. Try some turns

Hand Sliding

Rating: ♦♦♦♦♦

Hand sliding, also called power sliding and Bert sliding, looks super cool. Skaters of the 1970s wanted to emulate Larry Bertlemann, a famous surfer at the time. Bertlemann would stylishly place one hand on the open wave face when surfing, so a "Bert slide" is when you place your hand down on the cement while power sliding on a skateboard up a bank, ditch or flatland. When using a power slide while riding downhill, you do the same basic body maneuver while using a slide glove. This is called a Coleman slide, named after Cliff Coleman, the master downhill slider from the 1970s.

where you get down into that low position. Once you're comfortable with that,

put your hand out (with your slide glove on!) and let it skim over the surface of the road. Keep working on this trick, each time applying more and more pressure with your hand until you can slide the board so it's heading uphill again, which will bring you to a complete stop.

For corners, start by grabbing your board with one hand behind your front foot and placing the other on the ground. Lean hard toeside and get

the glove sliding first, then allow your wheels to slide slightly, scrubbing (losing speed). Try both backside and frontside (toeside and heelside). For frontside, grab the deck around your rear knee in front of your back foot. For every pound of pressure that you put on your hand, you're taking a pound off of your wheels, allowing them to break loose. Experiment with how much of your weight you need to throw in order to break the wheels loose.

GET SPONSORED

So your skills are super sick and your friends keep telling you to get sponsored. Being sponsored means that a company gives you free swag and money to skate. Sounds good, right? So how do you get this elusive sponsorship?

Enter contests. The best way to expose yourself and find out how good you really are is to compete against other girl skaters. Enter any and all contests in your area. Chances are, if you *are* really that good, the skateboard companies will come and find you. All Girl Skate Jam contests are renowned for having connected a lot of pro and amateur girls with their first sponsors ever.

Make a video of yourself. Work with your talented filmmaker friends and make a video or podcast of yourself doing some super-sick tricks. This is great to have on hand to give out to skate reps or send with a letter to skate companies. A photo disk works just as well, or post your photos online—this works as your promo card. Don't worry too much about the quality of the video or photos. If your skating is high quality, we promise that will shine through.

Trade Shows. Head out to the ASR (Action Sports Retail) tradeshow (asrbiz.com), which takes place twice a year in San Diego, California, and offers the latest on skateboards, apparel, shoes and companies. It's a great place to promote yourself.

Get an agent. An agent or business manager can help you book commercial try-outs, photo shoots, or speaking engagements. They can receive 10 to 30 percent of the profits you receive. Keep an email dialogue with your agent of updated photos of your skate tricks, portraits and contest winnings. All of this is ammunition for your agent to share with potential sponsors and/or jobs, so you want to keep your agent stoked. But keep in mind that you're not your agent's only client, unless you work out a special agreement from the start.

Helpful hint: Say the skate brands come knocking on your door. Please don't sign a contract with a company, agent or attorney without having a legal representative review it. If you're under 18, your parents will have to sign on your behalf. Bottom line is that rushing into a contract just because you're excited to get a sponsor or an agent is a bad deal. If the person that's giving you the contract can't wait for you to have someone legally review it, this is a red flag!

But before you get in over your head, JUST SKATE and have fun. Enjoy skating for what it is. Remember: Don't rush into becoming a pro and or marketing yourself like a Hollywood jock. Skate because you love it, okay?

Part 3:
Final Words

Chapter 6:
Be Safe, Play Smart

Okay, so cruising cement sidewalks and bombing asphalt hills with no airbags on your ride is a wee bit on the dangerous side. When we talk about safety we're talking about looking out for ourselves, but as skaters we also need to consider others. That's where etiquette comes into play. Etiquette, simply stated, means having good manners. You need to skate safe and smart to keep yourself and others on the street and out of the doctor's office.

SAFETY FIRST

Let's face it: Skateboarding can be a dangerous activity. You've heard people say, "If you're not falling, you're not learning," and it's true. You're gonna bail and inevitably get minor cuts and bruises, but the trick is to take precautions to get the most out of your skating experience with the least amount of "ow." Here are some no-brainers that will help you become the most successful skater you can be—safely!

Ageism.

Skateboarding is not recommended for children under the age of five. At this age, kids' bodies do not yet have the necessary balance. Children between five and ten years old should be supervised by an adult when skateboarding.

Wear your protective equipment.

Make sure to purchase protective equipment when you buy your first skateboard. Think of it as an entire package: if you have the board but not the gear, then you literally don't have what it takes to become a skater girl. You need to

>>> Don't forget there are instructional DVDs that show how to do most tricks. Aside from viewing these DVDs, you must actually practice the tricks over and over in order to land them.

take safety seriously, so always strap on that helmet and pull on those pads before stepping onto your skateboard—this is non-negotiable. Your helmet can save your life, or at least save you a big headache if your head connects with something hard. In addition to your helmet, wrist guards and knee and elbow pads can greatly reduce the chance of sprains, fractures or other nasty injuries. Like Goldilocks, you don't want your helmet and pads to be too big or too small—they need to fit just right to give you maximum protection while skating.

Check out the pros—they always have on protective gear when trying a new trick or skating a new spot. Almost every skate park requires skaters under the age of 18 to wear a helmet and pads at all times. And depending on what state you live in, you may be required *by law* to wear a helmet. Go online to check the skateboarding laws in your state before you head out.

Make sure you have high-quality equipment.

It's important to have a well-built skateboard—don't try to buy a cheap board from a toy store. Cheap skateboards are more likely to have hidden product defects that could cause the board to break during normal use. Wouldn't it be a bummer to crash just because the cheap plastic bolts on your trucks broke? Your pads and helmet should also be top of the line, and they have to be designed to fit *you*. If holding out for high-quality equipment means you need to save your pennies a little bit longer, it'll be well worth the wait.

Once you have a quality board and protective gear, make sure to take good care of them so that they keep taking care of you. Never leave your board, helmet or pads outside and subject to the elements. Check the bolts on your board every time you skate to make sure they haven't become loose, possibly causing your wheels to fall off. That would result in a gnarly fall. Take good care of your pads and helmet. If your equipment becomes damaged, replace it.

Never skate near traffic.

This is so important, we'll say it again: *Never skate near traffic*. A chance meeting with a car can leave you severely injured or even dead. So never, never, never skate on a busy street.

No towing.

Don't ever hold on to a moving vehicle such as a bus, car or even bike while on your skateboard. A free ride is just not worth the risk. Pro skater John Cardiel broke his back while being towed by a car.

Slippery when wet.

Everyone should experience skating on a rainy day—it's similar to going out snowboarding when it's snowing. You might want to use an old skateboard (a.k.a. a "rainboard") that you wouldn't mind getting wet. Just make sure to skate somewhere free of cars. Do be careful, as it will be very slippery as well as fun.

Night lights.

Don't skate at night. You won't be able to see your terrain clearly and cars won't be able to see you.

Fast friends.

Bring a buddy with you whenever you go skating. A buddy will help you face fears and encourage you to push yourself to be a great skater. It's also good

to have a friend around just in case anything goes wrong. A fellow skater girl can call your parents or contact the police in times of trouble.

Check it out.

Most injuries come from chance encounters with loose rocks or gravel, so scan the area before skating. Are there tree branches or potholes? If so, clear them out of the way or plan how to skate around them. (Tip: If you have a car, keep a broom in your trunk. This is a common practice among skaters.) Skate parks might be a better choice since their smooth surfaces are designed specifically for skating. Hopefully, they're free of debris, but

check out the skate park terrain before you drop in, especially if no one else is skating on it. Better safe than sorry!

Know how to fall.

It may sound stupid, but learn to fall *first*, before you start new tricks. As discussed in Chapter 4, knowing how to fall the right way can greatly reduce your chance of injury. Relax, stay low, and tuck and roll or run out of the trick if you're street skating. Try not to catch yourself with your hands or arms. If you put your hands out in front of you when you're falling fast, you could end up with a sprained or broken wrist. If you're skating a vert ramp or mini-ramp, you want to slide by falling to your knees. Falling is an unavoidable part of skateboarding, so learn to fall the *right* way.

How good are you *really?*

Know your skill level. Don't try tricks that are too advanced for you. For example, if you're just a beginner and still working up the courage to drop into a vert ramp, don't go for a 360 right away. Start small and move up. Master the basics before trying to wow the crowd with expert moves. One step at a time is the best way to get anywhere, especially when you're rolling on a board.

Stretch out.

Give yourself a good warm-up before skating. Skateboarding is a demanding activity and stretching ahead of time is a good way to prevent pulling or tweaking of uptight muscles. Check out Chapter 8 for recommended stretches that are easy to do before you hit the street.

Skate parks are great!

Skate parks are developed specifically for great skateboarding. They have smoother riding surfaces, better transitions, and are more likely to be monitored for safety than homemade ramps and jumps. That's why groups like the American Academy of Pediatrics and the US Consumer Product Safety Council recommend that communities develop more skate parks for kids.

Note to parents: Don't think of a skate park as a day-care center where you can just drop off your child and drive away. While skate parks are great places for children to skate, there isn't always a supervisor present to watch over

your little ducklings. If your child is young, stay with her at the skate park to keep an eye out and encourage her.

ETIQUETTE

While skateboarding has gotten a bad rap in the past, girl skaters can change that image by being kind and courteous to both civilians and other skaters. Alright, alright, we know skateboarding is all about expressing yourself and going hard, but at least try to avoid practicing your amazing handrail grind at the same time Grandma is coming up the stairs, y'know?

Here are a couple of thoughts to keep in mind before you head out and shred:

Pedestrians have the right of way. You're skating faster on your board than someone who's walking on their feet, so it's your job to avoid pedestrians, not the other way around. Be conscientious and thoughtful around others. This is especially important if you're coming up behind them, as they may unknowingly move in front of you at the last minute. Pass slowly.

Find your space. When learning to skate or trying out new tricks, make sure to practice in an unpopulated area. Don't ollie in the hallways of your school or office. This isn't just about your safety; it's about having concern for others and making sure your board doesn't fly up and hit them as you fall for the hundredth time.

Skate Park Etiquette

Unfortunately, there isn't a lot of fair play or etiquette in skateboarding. But here are a couple of polite things you can do at the park to keep yourself safe. These unwritten rules are necessary so that you don't crash into other skaters

and cause accidents and injuries. In fact, if you don't follow these rules, you may get thrown out of the skate park.

Scope it out. Take a look at all the park obstacles before taking on a new challenge. Which ramps or transitions do you know you can handle and which ones are brand-new to you? If you aren't familiar with something, watch how more experienced skaters handle it. Once you're sure you have the skills to try a piece of equipment, then you can head over to take it on.

Wait your turn. If you just drop into a bowl or ramp whenever you feel like it, you'll collide with other skaters and anger riders who are ahead of you. You must wait until the person on the ramp or bowl has completed the ride, either by kicking out or bailing. Once the skater ahead of you has cleared the way, it's your turn to go (as long as someone else hasn't suddenly dropped in ahead of you).

Intimidation tactics. We wish everyone would politely wait for his or her turn at the skate park, but you'll soon learn that this is not how it works. Being a girl has both advantages and disadvantages at a tough skate park. Some guys may let you go ahead of them in order to be chivalrous or to

encourage you. Others may play hardball and cut you off or never let you go. If this is the case, just know that they're insecure and feel sorry for them. If you're feeling timid and having a hard time getting a turn, go skate elsewhere in the park where it isn't as intense. When the crowd has thinned out or you're feeling more confident, go back to take on that first obstacle. Remember, the more you skate at a particular park, the more friends you can make there. Soon you'll be a regular and able to drop in whenever you want.

Drop in. In an ideal world, each skater would get one run and then wait in line until everyone else took his or her turn before getting a second run. But in the real world, there usually isn't an official line-up; it's the boldest skater who's going to go next. The first person to have a deck out, tail on the coping, is often the one who drops in next, no matter if other skaters are waiting. If you aren't the most aggressive skater at the skate park, it can be frustrating to have other skaters cut in ahead of you. Giving skaters puppy-dog eyes or a doubtful look isn't going to help; it's just going to tell stronger skaters that they can walk (or skate) all over you. Instead, scream out "Dropping!" and then drop in without hesitating. You have to be confident, assertive and, yes, some-what aggressive at a skate park if you want to drop in without getting repeat-edly snaked.

Help a girl out. Once you're good enough to drop in whenever the timing is right, watch out for other riders who may need help getting a turn before you jump back into the ramp. Especially look out for other girl riders who may be having a hard time. You were probably just like her once, so make sure she gets a chance.

No daisy chains. A "daisy chain" refers to the situation where you and your friends are at the park. One of you drops in, then another and another, and the next thing you know, your crew has taken over the whole ramp or bowl. If you and your friends are the only ones at the park, fine, If there are other skaters, you must share the equipment. No mob mentality, please.

No snakes. "Snaking" is when you drop in before it's your turn to skate. Severe snakes even drop in without waiting for the person ahead of them to finish. Snaking is uncool and mean. People aren't coming to the skate park to only watch you skate, so be cool and give others a chance to drop in and have fun. Skate friendly by allowing everyone to cruise around. For all you snakes reading this: You know who you are. If you aren't bringing positive vibrations to the skate park, then stay home until you can get into the flow.

Stand back. Always stand back from the edge of the ramp, pool or obstacle when you're watching other skaters. Keeping back by at least a whole body length will give you a safety zone in case other skaters lose their board while performing tricks. Always keep your eye on the skater's board in case it accidentally shoots out into the air. If you hear someone scream out "Board!" immediately cover your head with your arms and hands and tuck your head towards your body. Whenever you see a board flying into the air, it's a common courtesy to yell out "Board!" to warn others who don't know what's up and coming down fast.

Chapter 7:
Keep It Real

Being a skater girl is all in the attitude. That said, we mean a positive attitude.

Style. Create your own style of skating. It's totally up to you. Whatever works for you is the best way to skate, whether you decide to be a charging downhill skater, a mellow beach cruiser, an aggro street skater, or something in between. There's no right or wrong in skateboarding.

Imagine. Skateboarding is a pretty basic sport. Think about it: It's just the skateboard and you. So it's all about your creativity and how you see that sidewalk in front of you. A curb turns into something you can grind. A handrail becomes a slide. What kinds of things can you do when you get air? Sure, other skaters have come up with their own moves, but anything goes in skating. Make it up as you go along. Invent, innovate, improve. Be creative. We believe in you!

Skateboarding is all in your head.
Skateboarding is as much a mental challenge as it is a physical one, and the only thing stopping you from landing your trick is what's going on in your mind. If you hesitate or begin to doubt yourself, you're probably gonna eat it. But if you really, truly believe you can land a trick you've been practicing, you probably will.

In fact, you might want to try something called "ideokinesis," the mental practice of an activity—imagining movement in your mind and imagining your whole body performing it. Give this a shot: Close your eyes and envision yourself executing the perfect ollie. Imagine everything from the board under your feet, to snapping the tail of your board, to what it'll be like catching air, and then landing again. Dancers have long been using this method to teach their bodies routines. Once your body knows the move, it'll be much easier to perform it. Try it. It works!

Skateboarding is tough.
Skateboarding is a challenging sport to master. But want to hear some encouraging news? It's hard for everyone at the beginning or when learning new a trick. So don't let it bum you out when a trick isn't working or you're having a bad day. Remember back to the first time you got on a bike; everything takes practice to learn. The answer is perseverance—stick it out and hold on.

Practice, Practice, Practice! If at first you don't succeed, try, try again. It's like anything in life you do—the more you practice, the better you'll get. Many skaters have practiced tricks for what feels like a hundred times before they land them. Pro skater Cara-Beth Burnside always says, "You have to try a trick 50 times before you give up." You can excel in skating as long as you're willing to put in the time.

Be considerate. As mentioned in the etiquette section (page 87), make sure to be considerate of those around you. Don't be the girl who snakes everyone else in the skate park, or the girl who practices her ollies in the middle of a crowded courtyard. Practice, rip and shred. Just make sure you aren't doing it at someone else's expense.

Stay aware. Remember that you're a beginner and stay aware of yourself and those around you. Most accidents don't happen because of good skaters, they happen because mediocre skaters think they're better than they are. Don't be that girl and keep an eye out for other kooks out there.

You go girl! Encourage other girls. If you see other girls on the street or in the park, give them a smile and a yell of encouragement. Make friends and spread your influence by arranging a girl's night at your local skate park. Head out to all-girls contests, such as All Girl Skate Jam, to cheer on the pros and amateurs. At girls' contests you can meet a whole network of girl skaters.

Drop In. Whether it's physically dropping in on a ramp or mentally dropping into a scary situation, face your fears, drop in and go for it. Remember to take your abilities into consideration and only drop in on a ramp you're able to handle. Step up to the edge, push the board and your wheels over the coping and drop in. You'll get lots of speed and an adrenaline rush from dropping in and will soon want to experience the same feeling again.

No failure. You've probably heard the expression that success consists of getting up one more time than you fall. As long as you stand up, brush yourself off, and get back on the board, you'll never be a failure. Not being able to pull a trick should only inspire you to stick with it, try harder, and practice

longer. You may not be able to do a 900 in this lifetime, but sometimes just aiming for the lip is enough.

Hi there, hottie. Boys are an integral part of skateboarding, and we're big fans. But here's a thing or two to think about before falling for the hottie on the vert ramp. The absolute worst way to pick up a skater boy is by heading to the skate park when you have no business being there. Only go if you're going to skate or support a friend who's skating. A girl who hangs out at the skate park for no reason is called a "skate betty." Don't get us wrong—we want you at the skate park. We just want you to go there for *you*. The boys who see that you're a true skater girl just trying to improve will think you're way cool, even if you're still working on getting your pumping down on a ramp or tranny. Trust us.

If you've already nabbed yourself a skater boy, right on. Just make sure he supports your skating and helps you push yourself to be a better skater without pressuring you to try anything you aren't ready for. (Yes, we mean in more than just skating.)

Kiss the sky. We know you may just be a beginner, but we want you to get some air—at least mentally. Catching air is the ultimate stoke. You're flying, free and unbound. What could be better? Even if your wheels don't ever

As a skater girl, I promise to:

- Skate often.

- Give props to the other girl skaters out there.

- See the world as my oyster (unless that oyster has a "No Trespassing" sign on it).

- Face my fears, drop in and go for it.

- See failure as the ultimate motivation to succeed.

- Take only pictures and leave only footprints (or wheel marks, as the case may be).

- Keep it real.

leave the pavement, at least close your eyes, imagine yourself hitting the lip and soaring!

Tread lightly. Pick up after yourself, don't throw trash on the ground, and consider picking up other's trash on occasion. This may not seem like it belongs in a skater girl book, but we hope to make it every skater girl's philosophy. We all have to share this planet, so don't muck it up for yourself or others. Plus, how pissed would you be if you bailed because someone left their cigarette butt in the street?

And finally…

Don't be a poseur. If you're gonna skate, skate. It's totally cool to be a beginner and flail around. But don't be the girl who talks the talk without walking the walk. If your skateboard has been sitting in the garage for six months collecting dust, don't lie about the gnarly airs you just pulled. We love and encourage beginners, but don't fake it. Don't hang at the skate park pretending you're going to drop in but never do. It's okay to be scared and take it slow, but at least try. If you're trying, you'll never be a poseur in our book, even if you fall off every time.

Chapter 8:
Taking Care of the Whole Package—You!

No matter what your parents say, skateboarding is a sport and you'll need to be in good shape to pull those rail grinds you've been dreaming about. Being in shape starts from the inside. Eating well should be the basis of your healthy regime. Stretching will keep your muscles elastic and ready for action. Skating may feed your soul, but the asphalt can do a number on your skin—this chapter will also talk about first aid and caring for unsightly road rash.

DIET

Don't think by diet we mean for you to be on a weight-loss plan. What we're talking about is eating a wide assortment of whole foods that pack a ton of nutrition into each bite. As a skater girl, you're going to be burning calories like crazy, so make sure to fuel up with all-natural foods from all areas of the food pyramid.

Skip the prepackaged snacks and definitely skate on past the fast-food chains. Instead, grab a turkey sandwich on whole wheat bread, a cup of yogurt with low-fat granola, or a banana with some (natural) peanut butter.

Try to pick fiber-rich, whole wheat products over items made with white flour. Whole wheat offers more nutrition and studies show the fiber in it keeps you full longer.

Fruits and veggies are great choices for snacks. They taste great and also keep you healthy by fighting off disease. A food item that grows naturally is always a better choice than a food that is manufactured.

Protein is an important nutrient for anyone who's active, so make sure to fuel up

Smart Skater Girl Snack <<<

Here's a really easy snack idea that you can make for yourself and your friends after you come in from a hot skate session.

Skater Girl Slushy

½ fresh or frozen papaya (skin and seeds removed)

1 peeled banana

1 cup of cherry juice

2½ cups of ice

(optional) 1 nectarine

Place all ingredients in a blender and blend until smooth. Serves two thirsty skater girls.

with protein-rich foods such as lean cuts of meat, poultry, eggs and seafood. If you're a vegetarian, get your protein through nuts, beans or soy products.

Dairy products such as low-fat milk, cheese and yogurt have a lot of protein, too, and are also good sources of calcium, which is necessary for building strong bones—something every skater girl needs. Not a milk drinker? A number of milk alternatives such as soy milk and rice milk are fortified with calcium. Broccoli greens, kale and bok choy also pack a ton of calcium in each bite. Eww? All right, ice cream contains some calcium as well.

Everything is fine in moderation: chips, cookies, ice cream and cake—who can say no? Just make sure snacks or desserts are just that and you aren't eating chocolate cake for dinner.

Soft drinks are a waste of calories. Skip the soda and instead grab water or a sports drink like Cytomax or Gatorade. But be wary of sports drinks. Even though they offer more nutrition, they still have a lot of calories. Think about drinking only one a day instead of making it your drink of choice. Water should be your main thirst quencher.

STRETCHING

Skateboarding is hard on your body. You'll get a great workout, but your muscles will probably also become tight. Stretching will help keep you fit, your muscles flexible and lesson your chances of injury. For some super stretches that every skater girl can do, we contacted our friend Mark Rosenberg, D.C., creator of Howtostretch.com and chiropractor to many top professional skaters. Take a moment before and after each skate session to perform the following. Hold all stretches for 10 to 30 seconds. Never bounce to stretch further in any position—that was so 1980s.

Side Leg Stretch

If you have time to do just one warm-up before you drop in, this stretch is it. This opens up your hips and stretches your Achilles tendon, groin and hamstring.

Start by standing with your feet as wide as your outstretched arms. Your feet should be slightly turned out, about 45 degrees. Slowly bend your right leg, keeping your knee pointed over your toes. Place your hands on the floor, keeping as much weight on your hands as necessary. Slowly lower your hips until they're almost touching the ground, and roll your left foot so that your toes are pointed toward the sky. The extended leg should be  straight. Go slow. It's okay if your right heel comes off the floor because your Achilles tendon is tight. Come out of the position by rolling your left foot back down to the floor, straightening your body, and using your right leg to push up the rest of the way. Repeat on the other side.

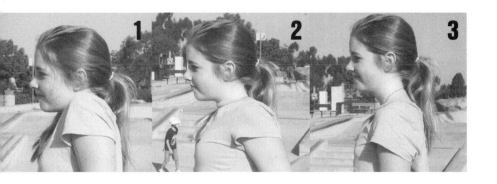

Neck and Shoulder Warm-Up

One more quick thing to do before you hop on your board is to warm up your neck and shoulders. To do this, roll your shoulders up and back a couple of times. Now roll them forward.

Do slow, gentle neck rolls by letting your head drop forward then to the side, gently back and to the other side. Keep your shoulders and the rest of your body still. Keep your mouth closed, and breathe through your nose.

Quadriceps Stretch

Standing on your left leg, bend you right knee and bring your right heel up to your butt. Hold on to your right foot with your right hand, keeping your left hand down or holding on to the wall or chair for balance. You should feel a nice stretch in the front of your upper leg. Try to keep your hips square and level; you absolutely shouldn't feel anything in your knee in this position. If your knee hurts, stop immediately. For a greater stretch, push your foot against your hand and start to bring the foot higher.

Seated Hamstring Stretch

Sit with your left leg straight out in front of you, foot flexed, and place your right foot against your left inner thigh. Relax your right knee to the ground. Keeping your back straight, slowly bend over your left leg and grasp your left calf, ankle or toes, depending on your flexibility. Look out over your left foot. You'll feel the stretch in the back of your leg. Don't let your head drop to your knee because doing so will round your back. Repeat on the other side.

Groin Stretch

While sitting, bring the bottoms of your feet together until they touch. Let your knees drop toward the floor. Keeping your back straight, hold on to your feet or ankles and lean forward from your hips. You should feel a nice stretch in your inner thighs, lower back and hips.

Standing Leg Stretch

This will stretch your back and hamstring muscles.

1 Stand with your feet wide and parallel to each other. Bend forward from your hips, keeping your hips level and your legs straight. Let your body hang; relax your head and neck. If you can, place your hands on the ground. This takes the weight and strain off your legs and back.

2 Now grab both ankles and gently pull yourself down a little more.

3 From here, reach over and hold your left ankle. Keep your hips level, your knees straight and your feet parallel. Hold the position, feeling the stretch in your leg and back. Release slowly, and move through the center to hold on to your right ankle. Repeat the stretch on the right side.

Squatting Hip Stretch

This is a good position to do after the standing leg stretch described above; it stretches the knees, hips, groin, Achilles tendons and sometimes the back. Start by standing with your feet shoulder-width apart and the feet turned out 45 degrees. Bend at your knees and lower your hips until they come down between your ankles. If you can't keep your heels on the ground, you may lift them up until the Achilles tendon and calf muscles stretch and relax. If balance is a problem, you can also hold on to a chair or wall until your heels touch the floor.

Downward Dog

This yoga pose will help strengthen your arms and stretch the backs of your legs. Start on your hands and knees, then straighten your arms and legs. Press your hips back so that most of the weight is in your legs. Think of your-self in an "L" shape, bent only at the hips, keeping your feet and hands flat on the floor. Your arms and legs should be straight, your head hanging down. If

your hamstrings are less flex-ible, you can keep your heels off the floor and/or your knees slightly bent. Keep your back nice and wide and try to keep your neck long so your shoulders aren't up around your ears. You can gently alternate straightening and bending your knees to feel a nice stretch up and down the backs of your legs.

Gentle Twist

Lie on the floor. Bend your knees and place your feet on the floor. Bring your arms out to either side. Keeping your upper back flat on the floor and your knees together, gently let your knees fall over to the left side. Reach out to the side with your right arm, pressing your right shoulder to the ground. You can place your left hand on top of your legs to give yourself a bigger stretch. This should feel awesome on your lower back. Change sides.

FIRST AID

Don't let this section freak you out. It's a good idea to have some first-aid knowledge before participating in any sports activity. Skateboarding can be totally safe when practiced properly, but since you're moving fast over concrete, it doesn't hurt to brush up on your first aid so that you or your buddy will be safe. By wearing your protective gear correctly, you'll minimize your chances of getting injured. Please remember, this is just a quick reference. You should seek medical attention for any and all serious injuries.

Bruises

We've all gotten them, and skater girls will get plenty more. When you fall or get hit with something, a bruise may form. This is caused by blood vessels breaking near your skin's surface, and the trapped blood may look like a black-and-blue mark or tiny red dots or splotches. Not to worry—while it may smart for a bit, a bruise will probably heal quickly on its own. A bruise may get darker after a couple of days but then should start to lighten and disappear. You can speed up the healing process by elevating the injured area and applying an ice pack.

If your bruise doesn't seem to be healing (for instance, if it doesn't go away or it gets worse and worse), you should see a doctor. You should also see a doctor if you start bleeding from your nose or gums, or if there's blood in your urine.

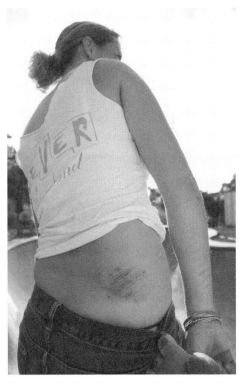

Concussion

Head injuries should always be taken very seriously. You should see a doctor if you've taken a serious fall and hit your head, even if you have no obvious symptoms. Symptoms of a concussion can include loss of consciousness, drowsiness, headache, blurred vision and/or seizures. If you hit your head and experience any of these conditions, call 911 or get to a doctor as soon as possible. If you were wearing your helmet when you fell, don't remove it. Leave it on, lay down and elevate your legs as you wait for medical help to arrive. If you're with a person who becomes unconscious for any amount of time, make sure to let the medical team know as soon as they arrive. Do not give the victim anything to drink, even if she complains of thirst.

Cuts and Scrapes

Here we're talking about the superficial abrasions you'll get when you take a spill on your board because, well, we all know concrete isn't exactly sympathetic. These cuts and scrapes hurt, for sure, but they aren't particularly deep and they stop bleeding quickly.

Stop the bleeding by applying gentle pressure with a clean cloth or bandage. Resist the urge to check on it since that may damage the clot that's forming and cause it to bleed again. (If the bleeding doesn't stop, consult a doctor.)

Rinse out the cut or scrape with soap and water. Since you may have skid across the asphalt, you may have dirt and debris in your cut. If it doesn't come out in the washing process, you can use sterilized tweezers. But if it still doesn't come out, seek medical attention.

Apply an antibiotic (like Neosporin or Polysporin) to the cleaned cut to keep it from getting infected. Cover the wound with a clean bandage and make sure to change the dressing daily or as it becomes dirty. If you notice the cut isn't

healing or there's redness, pus or swelling, consult a doctor.

Safety Note: If you're caring for a friend in need, be careful to avoid contact with blood or other bodily fluids. Wear latex gloves when treating others.

Dislocation

Dislocation is when a bone moves out of its normal position at a socket or joint. It can happen in large parts of your body such as your shoulder, knee, elbow or ankle, or even in small areas like your fingers or toes. You'll know if you dislocate something—it hurts! You may not be able to move the area of dislocation and it could look deformed. If during a fall you do feel that you dislocated something, seek medical attention as quickly as possible. Don't try to move the joint, but you can ice the area to reduce swelling.

Fractures

A fracture is a broken bone. If you suspect you broke something, go to the doctor or emergency room right away! Call 911 immediately if you or your friend is unresponsive, if there's heavy bleeding, or if the bone has gone through the skin. If there's bleeding, try to stop it by pressing on it with a clean cloth or a piece of clothing. Don't move the area of injury or try to bring the bone back into position—wait until medical help arrives. If your friend goes into shock (shortness of breath or fainting), lay her down with her legs elevated higher than her head.

Severe Bleeding

Let's avoid severe bleeding if we can. So no skating with sharp objects. No jumping off high places. But in the event that you tuck and roll into a sharp branch, here are some things to do. Lie down and keep the injured site elevated above the heart. Apply pressure to the wound until bleeding stops. If it does stop, wrap it tightly with a bandage or piece of clothing and head off to the hospital because a cut like this one will probably need stitches. If you or a friend were impaled (something is sticking out of you), don't pull the object out because it may be stopping the bleeding. Get to a hospital or call 911.

If the bleeding still doesn't stop after you've applied pressure and raised the injured limb, call 911 then apply pressure to the nearest main artery with your free hand as you continue to keep pressure on the wound itself. If your arm is injured, press on the inside of the arm between the elbow and armpit. Press the wrist if the hand is injured. Or if the injury is in the leg, use the heel of your hand and press firmly on the groin, on the crease between the leg and the pelvis. If it's lower on the leg, you can press behind the knee. Release the pressure points after the bleeding has stopped. Resume only if the bleeding will not stop.

Spinal Injury

Don't love this one, either. Again, remember to use precaution and know your abilities before you attempt any advanced tricks. Should you do something where you seriously injure your neck or back, you may lose consciousness, have serious pain in your neck or back, and/or feel numb in areas of your

body. Lie still. Don't move. Have someone call 911 right away and wait until help arrives. If there's also severe bleeding, try to put pressure on the wound without moving the rest of the body. If you're in a dangerous area, such as the street, and need to move an injured person, do so by moving the body as lightly as possible. Grab clothing and drag them as gently as possible without tweaking their back or neck. The goal is to keep the person still until medical help arrives.

Sprains & Strains

Sprains (overstretching or tearing ligaments, the tough bands of tissue that connect your bones to each other) and strains (overstretching or tearing of muscle) are, unfortunately, familiar ailments to the skater girl. The most common place for a sprain is your ankle, knee or finger; strains can occur in any muscle group, such as those in your arms, legs and back. Seek medical attention right away for a severe sprain or strain, but if you simply tweak your ankle or pull your calf muscle and it doesn't hurt too badly, you should follow the R.I.C.E. plan.

R Rest the injured area. If you continue to skate on it, you might make it worse.

I Ice the area. This will help control the swelling. Apply ice right away and go for 30 minutes on, 30 minutes off for the next 12 to 24 hours.

C Compress the area with a wrap or bandage.

E Elevate the area to reduce swelling.

If your sprain or strain doesn't start improving in two or three days, go see a doctor.

Tooth Loss

Should you take a face plant and end up looking like a pro hockey player (if you choose, you can wear a mouth guard when skating), gather up any teeth that have fallen out and seek medical help immediately. Doctors may be able to reimplant your permanent teeth but only if you act fast—30 minutes after the injury. Gently rinse the tooth/teeth in a bowl of cool water (running water could damage the tooth) and try to place it back in your mouth, biting down on a gauze to keep it in place. If that's not possible, place the tooth in milk or a warm saltwater solution. Again, get to the doctor or emergency room immediately.

Reminder: Your protective equipment will reduce risks of all the injuries listed above. Always wear your gear and be safe!

And one more thing...

Don't Smoke

There, we said it. Athletes shouldn't smoke and, if you're a skater girl, you're an athlete. We know that some of the skaters out there smoke and think it's a part of the skater lifestyle. But it's not. Smoking is gross, unfriendly to the environment (do you know how many cigarette butts end up in the ocean each year?) and can kill you. So why did you want to do it again?

Chapter 9:
Skateboarding:
A Girl's History

Skateboarding has risen and fallen in popularity since the day it was born. The style of skating has alternated as well—one decade street skating would be hot, while another decade vert skating would be the rage. But what hasn't changed is women's participation in the sport. Even though the number of girls who skate has gone from many to few and back, girls have always been a part of the movement.

PRE-1950s

There's no individual inventor of skateboards and no exact moment when the first skater stepped on the first skateboard. Skateboards were the brainchild of girls and boys all over the world, who created foot-powered fun with just a hard piece of wood, steel wheels and no bearings. They dismantled roller skates and nailed the wheels to planks of wood. They ripped the handlebars off their scooters so they could ride the decks.

The year 1959 saw the first commercial skateboard: the Roller Derby Skateboard. That same year, the film *Gidget*, about a Malibu girl who just wanted to hang out at the beach and surf, turned America on to surfing. But what does a surf flick have to do with the development of girls' skateboarding? Well, surfers learned pretty quickly that when they couldn't get out on the waves, they could always experience that same freedom by hitting the streets with their skateboards. Skateboarding was also known as "sidewalk surfing" because riders rode both the waves and cement in a similar style. The close-ness in movement made skating and surfing the perfect combination, and as

surfing grew in popularity, so did skateboarding. Existing surfboard companies were some of the first to hop aboard the skateboarding wagon. Companies such as Gordon & Smith and Hobie began to manufacture their own line of skateboards.

1960s

Although girls represented only a small percentage of early skateboarders out on the streets, they were definitely out there riding. The new styles of skating (slalom, downhill racing, and freestyle) contributed to their interest. The surf industry continued to push the sport of skateboarding. In 1963, the publisher of *Surf Guide*, Larry Stevenson, rolled skateboarding into the mainstream. Larry and his company, Makaha Skateboards, formed a professional skate team to promote his new product and exposed millions of kids around the country to skateboarding. Wendy Bearer, a member of Makaha's national team, became a role model for female skaters. To show off their new products, more and more skate companies followed Makaha's lead and began creating teams, hosting demonstrations and skateboard contests. These contests

Humble Beginnings

I think the year was 1962. We were riding 2x4s cut about 22 to 24 inches long with the metal skates nailed on. Don Hansen decided to make a Linda Benson and a LJ Richards model, shaped like a surfboard with our names stenciled on the tail block. The wheels were the best made at the time, a roller-rink type that we screwed on by hand in the back room of Hansen's Surfboards old shop in Cardiff. Bagged in plastic, I packed them up and went on a road trip up the coast all the way to Santa Monica, stopping at hardware stores, Pep Boys, etc.—there were no sporting goods stores at that time. I would walk into the store and show the new product and give a demonstration out on the sidewalk. Most people were amused, and I sold quite a few. *Art Linkletter's House Party*, a popular daytime variety show, invited us up to Hollywood to demonstrate the skateboard in CBS's parking lot. It was the start. —*Linda Benson, world champion surfer*

included all-girl divisions and pushed female skaters to improve. Girls especially excelled at freestyle, since their flexible bodies allowed them to perform gymnastic-like tricks on the boards.

The real revolution in skateboarding arose with the onset of new materials and design ideas. Larry Stevenson came up with the kicktail—an upward turn of the tail of a skateboard that made it easier to perform tricks; it can be seen on almost all modern decks. In 1964, Larry Gordon introduced the Fiberflex skateboard, which was made of fiberglass and wood and was more responsive to the rider's movements and retained its shape better than the early plywood boards. These innovations were the start of many that would improve the quality of skateboards.

In 1965, just when the cover of *Life* magazine featured national women's champion Pat McGee doing a handstand on a skateboard, the public and police started to shut skateboarding down. Due to a high number of injuries, skateboarding was outlawed in public places. As soon as it boomed, skating almost disappeared completely. Skateboards were taken off store shelves, and those who wanted to continue with the sport had to make their own boards again.

1970s

The skateboarding boom began again in 1973, when Frank Nasworthy and his company Cadillac Wheels introduced urethane wheels. Almost all the early skateboards had clay wheels with no grip, which meant that the second you hit even a small pebble, you went down. Urethane, a resilient and gripping new material, would change the face of skateboarding. These wheels were a tough sell at first because of their high price tag, but skaters soon caught on. Adding bearings made the wheels run faster and smoother. With the innovation in wheels, skate companies realized it was time to make a truck specifically for skateboarding. Bennett, Tracker and Independent led the way in improving skateboarding conditions.

>>> In 1978, Alan Gelfand invented the "ollie," the maneuver in which you step down on the tail of your board, get air while keeping your feet on the board, and land—all without using your hands. The ollie would become one of the keystones in the skateboarder's arsenal of tricks. Alan was only 14 years old at the time. How cool is that?

A wave of female skaters hit the streets in the '70s and could be seen all over the country. Laura Thornhill, a leading skater of the time, won contests in Slalom Freestyle and Overall categories and was one of the first female skaters to have her own signature skateboard. California girl Ellen O'Neal, who rode for Gordon & Smith, was the Free Former world champion; she was known for her daffys, a maneuver where the rider performs wheelies on two boards. Other female riders included Ellen Berryman, who specialized in gymnastics and was sponsored by Bahne Skateboards; Robin Logan, who was the first woman to do a kickflip; Desiree Von Essen, a top female skater who starred in the 1976 feature film *Freewheelin'*; and Kim Cespedes, who rode for Hobie Skateboards and was featured in *Skateboarder Magazine* for her impressive bank skating.

In the early '70s, skaters were still doing tricks from the '60s. Gymnastics such as the L-sit (holding on to the board and piking your body), slaloming, handstands and jumps were still the standard tricks at contests. The second half of the '70s saw the introduction of a whole new style of skating—vert, an abbreviation for "vertical." Although there's evidence of riders skating empty swimming pools as early as 1965, because of the 1976 drought in California, more and more swimming pools were emptied and skaters were dropping in, invited or not. That same year, the first of many skate parks was opened in Florida, leading to a rise in a new kind of skateboarding. Because skaters could now go vertical and actually ride out of the pool or ramp ("getting air"), skateboarding turned into something entirely different. Vicki Vickers, Pattie Hoffman (who was on the Pepsi skate team) and Teri Lawrence embraced this new vertical style and became well-known female vert skaters. Do remember that equipment was an issue in these early days of skateboarding. Skaters didn't have high-tech protective equipment like we do today. Imagine bailing on a vert ramp without proper knee pads—these skaters were particularly brave!

The Zephyr team from Dogtown (Santa Monica, CA) was at the crux of this new style. Zephyr, a surfboard manufacturing company run by Jeff Ho, Craig Stecyk and Skip Engblom, sponsored surfers such as Tony Alva, Jay Adams and Stacy Peralta, who would later become members of the infamous skate-

board team. When Zephyr saw the potential of urethane wheels, they created their own skateboard design that integrated a rocker (a gentle curve to the board). At the 1975 Bahne-Cadillac Ocean Festival in Del Mar, California, the crew was revealed to the skating world. These Dogtown skaters introduced a whole new vocabulary to the once-sedate skating community. Slaloming, gymnastics and wheelies gave way to grinding, Berts and airs. Peggy Oki, the sole female member of the Zephyr team, won first place in the Women's Freestyle division. You can see more about the Zephyr team in the documentary *Dogtown and Z-Boys* or the feature film *Lords of Dogtown*.

1980s

The end of the 1970s suffered the same fate as the '60s. Insurance costs and safety concerns closed the doors of many of the skate parks, and by the 1980s bulldozers were wheeling through the skate parks instead of girl skaters. Skateboards were being left in the garage as kids picked up a shiny new toy, the BMX bike. *Skateboarder Magazine* became *Action Now* and featured a range of sports.

Skateboarding went underground in the early 1980s and turned decidedly punk and overwhelmingly male. The first issue of *Thrasher* was published in

1981; their motto was "Skate and Destroy." This male-dominated magazine was geared toward hardcore skaters, and skateboarding became a subculture linked with anarchy. If women wanted to compete, instead of skating with other women as they had in the past, they had to go up against the men in competitions. Vert skating reigned, and if you weren't catching air, you could practically hang up your board for good. It was down and dirty and only a few women held on during this time.

As the '80s rolled on, skateboarding began to veer back toward the mainstream. Skate videos were everywhere and the public's interest began to peak again. Professional skaters were becoming media darlings. The National Skateboarding Association, formed in 1983 by Frank Hawk (Tony Hawk's dad), was the first organization to be supported by all the major skateboard companies; it began holding contests worldwide. *Transworld Skateboarding*, a tamer skate magazine, was first published in 1984. It was now possible to make a living as a skateboarder by promoting new skate fashion lines such as Vans, Vision and Airwalk. Skaters and non-skaters alike were dressing the part.

In 1989, Laura Medlock created the Women's Skateboard Network, which was further snowballed by University of California at San Diego student Lynn Kramer. The Network consisted of more than 250 girls from five countries. The girls kept up with each other through the 'zine *Equal Time* (its motto: "no nuts, just guts"), which was founded by Lynn in 1988 and sustained by girl skaters

The Birdman

It's hard to talk about skateboarding without mentioning Tony Hawk. Tony is handsome, totally likeable and has made skateboarding respectable (although he'd probably hate to admit that). Tony got on his first skateboard when he was nine years old and was known as the world's best skateboarder by age sixteen. At the 1999 Summer X Games, Tony Hawk pulled the first 900 (two-and-half revolutions in the air) ever seen at a competition. Tony has a company called Birdhouse Skateboards, a clothing line called Hawk, and a handful of video games for PlayStation. Plus, Tony's a big supporter of women's skateboarding. What's not to like?

Hazardous to Your Health?

For years, there's been a movement to turn skateboarding into an official "Hazardous Recreational Activity" in every state (it's already recognized as an HRA in 14 states). Having HRA status means that you take responsibility for yourself while performing a hazardous activity and cannot hold others (such as a city or skate park) responsible. BMX biking and many other activities such as inline skating are already labeled HRA in some states. While this sounds like a bad thing, it'll actually allow more skate parks to open by keeping insurance costs down since the skate parks won't be held responsible for injuries sustained while skateboarding. Skateboarders have refused to sue for more than 25 years, and because of this, many cities are building skate parks based on this act of good faith. More than 500 skate parks exist around the country as of this printing.

who would submit articles and photos of themselves. In 1992, Lynn handed off the 'zine to Joann Gillespie and the Women's Skateboard Network. Top skaters featured in *Equal Time* included Lynn Kramer, Cara-Beth Burnside, Saecha Clarke, Anita Tessensohn, Lisa Foreman, Nathalie Richter, Patty Segovia, Stephanie Person, Christy Jordahl, Lori Rigsbee, Vicky Voughn, Joanne Gillespie and Chris Reis, among others. The photos and stories in the 'zine inspired girls to skate harder.

1990s

And then it happened again. The recession of the early 1990s caused the skate industry to take a big hit. The bottom dropped out and it was tough for professional skateboarders to make a living. The skateboard companies that did survive aimed their marketing almost exclusively toward teenage boys. Rollerblading became the sport *du jour*. Skate parks began closing again, and skaters were back on the street. This caused vert to go out of fashion and street skating to become cool again. Some vert skaters who rocked the ramps found themselves floundering when trying to pull simple street maneuvers.

As the recession started to lift, "extreme sports" such as skateboarding, BMX, snowboarding and motocross became the new rage. In 1995, ESPN broadcast these sports across the world with the first Extreme Games (now known as the X Games). Soon everyone was trying to jump on board and in 1999, the Gravity Games, NBC's answer to the X Games, offered the world yet another glimpse at extreme sports.

Women's skating began to reemerge at the end of the 1990s. Taking the lead from women's snowboarding, women began to pull together and support each other. In 1997, the All Girl Skate Jam held its first all-girl competition with a prize purse, giving women more opportunity to skate together, encourage each other, and inspire others to try skateboarding.

2000s

Skateboarding is back big time and women are charging. Step aside, watch out and "excuse me while I kiss the sky." More and more girls are stepping onto boards every day. The decade so far has been a good one for female skaters. The X Games and Gravity Games both created women's divisions in vert and street skateboarding. Magazines and 'zines featuring women's extreme sports such as Check It Out and Second Wind, as well as online sites The Side Project and Girls Skate Better, are popping up everywhere. All-girl contests and clinics, inspired by the All Girl Skate Jam, are happening around the world.

Cara-Beth Burnside, Elissa Steamer, Vanessa Torres, Heidi Fitzgerald, Jen O'Brien and others have set the bar high and more and more girls are stepping up to the challenge.

Judi Oyama, a premiere <<< slalom and downhill skater in the 1970s, found herself competing again in 2001 at the "Battle on the Bay" giant slalom race. For her first-place win, she received exactly what she had received 20 years ago: $0 (although she had to pay $100 just to enter the race!). Sadly, in some events women are still not receiving the recognition or respect they deserve today.

The competition of girl skaters is getting younger and stronger. Look to girls like Lauren Perkins, Apryl Woodcock and Lyn-z Adams Hawkins to raise the level of girls skating everywhere—Hawkins amazingly landed the 55-foot DC Mega Ramp at the age of 15.

Now there's talk of skateboarding becoming an Olympic sport at the 2008 Olympics in China. Skaters are petitioning the Olympic Committee to have women included in the demo. Keep your fingers crossed and get out there and make some history yourself!

The All Girl Skate Jam: A Message from Patty

I'm passionate about helping girls excel in skating. In 1990, I organized the first all-girl skate demonstration. Why? Because there wasn't a place where girls could go and compete at a skateboard event. At that point, girls' skating events or even girls' skateboard divisions at boys' contests were nonexistent. For years, all I heard from other guys and skateboard industry people was "Girls can't skate" or "Girl skaters don't deserve to be paid."

By 1996, I knew a void still existed in the girls' skateboarding world so I created the first-ever event with a prize purse for the girls. The All Girl Skate Jam (AGSJ) awarded $3,750 for vert and street disciplines—the highest paying cash purse in the history of girls' skateboarding. Contestants from Canada, Brazil, Japan and Switzerland came all the way out to San Diego, California—imagine the great efforts and sacrifices these girls made just to skate. I'll never forget the call from Fox TV asking me if they could send down a crew. ESPN2 and lots of other press were present as well. Major magazines and journalists came to write about history in the making. Through this event, and via TV, magazines and international satellite feed, skater girls would be exposed to the world.

The AGSJ movement arose out of demand and helped place girls' skateboarding on the map. The AGSJ is the first and only skateboarding competition for girls of all ages and of all abilities. Competition includes both amateur and professional levels. To date, AGSJ has grown to award $5,000 and $7,500 prize purses. By providing a unique competitive series devoted solely to women, the AGSJ brings women of the new millennium together and allows one-on-one interaction. The competition was originally an annual event, but the popularity and demand from women skaters is so great that the AGSJ is also involved in action and extreme sports events around the world. The AGSJ runs skate clinics for beginning skaters in all 50 states as well, and offers a skate/surf camp every summer.

Skater girls from all around the world have sacrificed traveling to the AGSJ events because they love to skate and know that the AGSJ rolls out the red carpet for them. In an interview for ESPN, Tony Hawk remarked, "The AGSJ allows the girls to shine in the limelight and not get lost in the mix."

GLOSSARY

Please note: Skateboarding is all about freedom and personal expression so keep in mind that a definition may have more than one specific meaning.

Acid drop To skate off a high ledge and land on the ground on all four wheels. (Beware of injury to knees and ankles!)

Air When you and your skateboard no longer have contact with the ground and experience an elated feeling of weightlessness. Sometimes short for "aerial."

Axle stall To ride up a transition, place both trucks on the coping or edge, pause for a moment and then ride back down. Also known as a 50-50 stall.

Backside When your back is facing the obstacle, wall, wave or transition as you perform a trick. Opposite of *frontside*.

Bail To jump off your board right before you're about to land a trick—a cautious thing to do when you don't feel 100% on your board. (Jumping off your board too often may earn you the title of "Bail Queen" so you may just want to stick it—land it already!)

Bank A slanted wall (usually made of cement) that is less than 90 degrees. You can find these around parking lots, irrigation ditches or playgrounds. These are fun because you can practice tricks on banks and later take the tricks you master onto a *mini-ramp* or *vert ramp*.

Baseplate The flat plate that attaches the truck to the deck of the skateboard.

Bearings The hardware containing ball bearings that goes inside of your skateboard wheels and allows them to turn.

Blank A plain skateboard deck with no graphic design.

Blunt To go up to the transition on a ramp and, keeping your skateboard vertical, locking your tail or nose against the coping with a stall, wheels on top of the obstacle, and smoothly coming back into the ramp.

Board (or Deck)   The top of the skateboard that your feet ride on. Usually made of wood, although some are made from other materials like plastic.

Boardslide   When you slide your skateboard along a coping, rail or piece of wood by turning it horizontally and sliding on the bottom side of the deck. These are super fun on a shiny, red, two-sided cement curb. Also known as a railslide (on any kind of rail).

Bomb   To go downhill fast.

Caballerial   Steve Caballero invented this trick where the skater on a vert ramp performs a fakie 360-degree spin in the air with no grab.

Carve   To make long S-turns by alternately putting pressure on your toes and heels.

Concave   The scoop in the skateboard deck. The concave strengthens the board and helps with certain tricks such as ollies and airs.

Coping   The metal, cement or plastic pipe along the lip of the half-pipe, bowl or pool.

Crooked grind   When you grind along your nose trucks with the back trucks purposely off the equipment. This adds style to your grind and is very common in street skating. Also known as K-grind.

Drop in   To begin a ride by leaning forward and skating down from the top of a ramp or pool.

Durometer   This measures the hardness of a skateboard wheel.

Face plant   When you land face first on the pavement or wooden floor. Ouch!

Fakie   Riding backwards.

Feeble grind   When your back truck grinds on coping while your front truck is off the edge, putting you at a slight angle. Trick tip: Point your front toe to help lock the feeble grind in place.

50-50 grind   Grinding with both trucks along an object.

Frontside   When your front is facing the obstacle, wall, wave or transition as you perform a trick. Opposite of *backside*.

Goofy foot   When your natural position is to stand on a board with your right foot forward.

Grab   To grab the skateboard with one or both hands while in the air or performing a trick.

Grind   To slide along the coping, curb, handrail or other object on your trucks. Should create a loud, crispy, grinding noise.

Grip tape   The sandpaper-like material that sticks to your deck, helping your feet grip the board.

Half-pipe   A U-shaped ramp.

Hand plant   A one-armed handstand done while bending your knees into your chest and holding the board to your feet (also known as an invert).

Hanger   The metal part of the truck that covers the axle. This is the part of the board you grind on.

Heelflip   While ollie-ing, pressing down on your heel to flip the board underneath your feet, then landing it. Opposite of a *kickflip*.

Kick turn   To rotate 180 degrees on your back wheels, turning your body and skateboard at the same time. Kick turns are usually done to return to where you originated.

Kicker   A small or big launch ramp that allows you to catch air. You usually see kickers in skate parks or outside of homes on sidewalks. You can practice tricks on kickers and take them to bigger obstacles.

Kicktail   The tail of your board that comes up at an angle.

Kickflip   When ollie-ing, pressing down on your toe to flip the board underneath your feet. Opposite of a *heelflip*. This is a standard basic trick for a pro skater. It's the essence of tricks such as double kickflips or kickflips to fakie (different variations).

Kingpin   The bolt that holds the hanger and axle to the base plate.

Kneeslide   A ramp maneuver where the skater tries to lessen the impact of a fall by sliding on her knees (which are covered with kneepads!).

McTwist   A 540-degree spin performed on a ramp. Invented by Mike McGill. Also known as a 540.

Mini-ramp   A half-pipe that is generally under eight feet with no vertical.

Nollie   To ollie by pushing down on the nose of your skateboard.

Nose   The front portion of your deck or board.

Nosegrind   To grind with your front truck (meaning the truck closest to the front of the board) along an edge, coping or curb.

Noseslide   To slide along an obstacle using the nose (front) of your board.

Ollie   To get air on your skateboard by putting pressure on the tail of your board, leveling off in the air and landing without using your hands to hold the board. Invented by Alan Gelfand.

Pumping   To gain momentum on a ramp by compressing and shifting your weight (much like what you would do on a swing).

Pushing   To push off your back foot while riding to gain momentum.

Quarter-pipe   Half of a half-pipe.

Regular foot   When your natural position is to stand on a board with your left foot forward.

Session   Time of skateboarding, or to skate together with friends. A "heated session" means skating hard non-stop for hours. The more warmed up you are, the more daring you get and begin to try new tricks and get egged on by your friends to "land it" or "do it."

Skate tool   This tool, used specifically for putting together or maintaining skateboards, usually includes a wrench, screwdriver, socket and bearing press. Sometimes known as a skate key.

Stalled   To pause in the middle of a trick, either to prepare for the next trick and acquire better balance, or for stylish reasons.

Switch stance   To skate with your unnatural foot forward. If you're right-handed it would be like writing left-handed, only you're skating left-footed. Get it? Skaters sometimes change foot positions in the middle of a trick, gaining them more points in a contest.

Tabletop   The flat surface of a jump. (Don't land here or you'll buckle or strain your ankles!)

Tail   The back end of your deck (board), which has a scoop to it.

Tailslide   To slide along an obstacle using the tail (back) of your board.

Transition   The gentle slope between the flat and vertical on a half-pipe, ramp or pool. Also known as tranny.

Truck   The metal hardware shaped like a T that holds your wheels onto your board. The bearings and wheels are connected to the outside screws of the trucks. Trucks are both solid and durable and allow for long, hard grinds.

Vert   Short for "vertical." Perpendicular to the horizon or 90 degrees.

Vert ramp   A half-pipe that is usually 11 feet or more in height.

Wall   Another name for vertical. A super gnarly wall where you have to suck your knees up to your chest in order to defy gravity so that you can pull off the wall ride or trick.

Wheelie   When you're balanced on your board with either your front or back wheels in the air.

Wheels   Skateboard wheels are normally made up of a urethane material and allow your skateboard to roll.

BIBLIOGRAPHY

Books

American Medical Association. *Handbook of First Aid and Emergency Care*, Revised Edition. New York: Random House, 2000.

Brooke, Michael. *The Concrete Wave: The History of Skateboarding*. Toronto, Canada: Warwick Publishing Inc., 2003.

Cackett, Joanne. *Great Aussie Sports: Skateboarding*. Sydney, Australia: Echidna Books, 2005.

Davis, James. *Skateboarding Is Not a Crime: 50 Years of Street Culture*. New York: Firefly Books, Inc., 2004.

Morgan, Jed. *No Limits: Skateboarding*. London: Franklin Watts, 2005.

Werner, Doug. *Skateboarder's Start-Up: A Beginner's Guide to Skateboarding*. San Diego: Tracks Publishing, 2000.

Magazine Articles

La Rochelle, Sasha. "Judi Oyama." *Surf Life for Women*. Summer 2005.

Owen, Arrissia. "Girls Skate: A Select History of the Industry." *Wahine Magazine*. April 2000.

Porter, Natalie. "Female Skateboarders and Their Negotiation of Space and Identity." *Journal for the Arts, Sciences, and Technology*, Vol. 1, No. 2 (2003).

Web Articles

American Academy of Pediatrics. "Skateboard and Scooter Injuries." Vol.109, No. 3 (March 2002): 542-543. http://www.aap.org/healthtopics/safety.cfm.

Bicycle Helmet Safety Institute. "Helmets for Many Activities: Skateboarding Helmets." http://www.bhsi.org/other.htm#skateboard.

Cave, Steve. "Just Starting Out Skateboarding." About.com. http://skate board.about.com/od/tricktips/ss/JustStartingOut.htm.

————. "A Brief History of Skateboarding." About.com. http://skateboard.about.com/cs/boardscience/a/brief_history.htm.

EXPN.com. "Skateboarding Glossary." http://expn.go.com/glossary/skt/index/html.

Mayo Clinic Staff. "First Aid Guide." MayoClinic.com. http://www.mayoclinic.com/findinformation/firstaidandselfcare/index.cfm.

Rosenberg, Mark. "Stretches." Howtostretch.com. www.howtostretch.com.

"Skateboard Dictionary." http://www.geocities.com/Pipeline/Slope/4774/sk8dictionary.html.

Skateboard.com. "Skateboard 101: My Ride." http://www.skateboard.com/frontside/101/myride.

U.S. Consumer Product Safety Commission. "Skateboarding." Consumer Product Review, Vol. 7, No. 4 (Spring 2003). http://www.cpsc.gov/cpscpub/pubs/cpsr_nws28.pdf.

U.S. Consumer Product Safety Commission. "Skateboards," Publication #93. http://www.cpsc.gov/cpscpub/pubs/093.pdf.

Wanner, Noel. "Skateboard Science: The Science and Art of Skateboard Design." Exploratorium.edu. http://www.exploratorium.edu/skateboarding/skatedesign.html.

SHOUT OUTS

Patty Segovia: My dad Ysaias, for giving me the confidence to write this book; he always told me, "Anyone can write a book!" My mom Maria, for putting her words into actions, for demonstrating that anything is possible and for her wonderful sense of humor. My loving sister Rachel, who has gotten down and dirty at many AGSJ events. My other loving sister Cindy, for always praying for me. My partner in vida Kervin Krause, for his endless support; peaceful, loving approach; and organizational skills. Our dogs Nina and Stoli and cats Trippy and Zippy, for helping me see the Zen in life. My beloved Uncle Willie, who gave me love and support throughout my life, RIP. Last but not least, la abuelita, for holding my hand.

World Slalom Champion Lynn Kramer, for her endless skate trick revisions; Joann "Rawkmom" Gillespie; Isabelle Caudle; nomads Heidi Fitzgerald and (Jimmy the Greek) Marcus—my honor to have their expertise in photo editing for this book; Cara-Beth Burnside, for her inspiration; Tony Alva; Damon Meibers/What Design; co-author Rebecca Heller; Steve Van Doren; Kevin Lyman; Todd Peterson; Dagmar Krause; Jeff Endlich; Laura Thornhill; Warren Bolster; Michael Bream; Mike Taylor; my AGSJ staff, Kathy Espejo, Chris Dumas; Simone Campbell; Kaysie Whitehead; Eric Swank; AGSJ skater girls; Brad Smith; Mark Williams; Pam Rittlemeyer; Paper; Kate Nelligan/ESPN X Games; Heidi Lemon; Paul Swank; Spotty; and, most of all, Dios.

Rebecca Heller: Kevin Buchli, Cara-Beth Burnside, Kate DeBlasio, Skip Engbloom, Heidi Lemmon, Stef McDonald, Mark Rosenberg, D.C., Patty Segovia, and Debra Stein.

Both authors would like to thank all at Ulysses Press, especially Ashley Chase, for first contacting us about writing this book; Bryce Willett, an ex-punk skater from the '70s whose knowledge of skateboarding helped make this book better; Ray Riegert and Lily Chou.

Thanks also to the photography models: Juliann and Bethany Andreen, Meredith Betts, Cara-Beth Burnside, Isabelle Caudle, Kim and Elly Cherryholmes, Amelia Croeka, Ciara D'Agostino, Lucianna Ellington, Heidi Fitzgerald, Lynn Kramer, Lorena Lima, Gwen Marcus, Aliza Montes, Ameejay Papelera, Ally Rosenberg, Kristi Sanders, Patty Segovia, Jessica Starkweather, Annie Sullivan, Lindsi Thompson, Apryl Woodcock, Leilani Marques, Amber Lorentzen, Nikki Likenn, Cressey Rice, Simone Campbell, Candy Hiler, Judith Rogers, Charlie Moehr, Andrea Mohrle, Amy Allen, Liz Stockholm, Laura Thornhill, Jen O'Brien, Jodi McDonald, Leslie Olson, Melissa Spillman, Michelle McKinsley, Heidi Kreis, Sonya Claudhill, Olivia Rhode, Julie Kindstrand, Candice Starin, Jewels, Kim Peterson, Elissa Steamer, Amber Cangoliose, Lyn-Z Adams Hawkins, Caylin Dakin, Sunny Elizabeth, Vanessa Torres, Alexis Schemp, Vienna Torres, Carlee Torres, Kaity Elizabeth, Canan Omer, Cody Malia Peer and Mimi Knoop.

ABOUT THE AUTHORS

Patty Segovia, the founder of the All Girl Skate Jam, directs the AGSJ on a 50-city tour every year (you can catch the AGSJ events on Fox Fuel TV and ESPN2). A photographer, producer, agent, skater and author, she has been featured in many national magazines, including *Latina* and *Time*. She frequently shoots for *Sports Illustrated for Women* and the *New York Times*, and has written several other books including *On the Edge: Snowboarding and On the Edge: Skateboarding* and *Skate Girls*.

Rebecca Heller is the author of *Surf Like a Girl: The Surfer Girl's Ultimate Guide to Paddling Out, Cathing a Wave* and *Surfing with Aloha*. She continues to keep girls stoked through her online web 'zine, Surflikeagirl.net, dedicated to girls who surf, skate and snowboard. In the warm months, she teaches women of all ages to surf. She lives in Los Angeles and is still trying to find room for all her surf, skate and snowboards.